The
Vegan
Epicure

135 Delicious Recipes for Healthy Eating

The Vegan Epicure

135 Delicious Recipes for Healthy Eating

HERMINE FREED

Sterling Publishing Co., Inc
New York

Metric Equivalents for Recipes

1 cup = 240 ml
1 Tbsp = 3 tsp = 15 ml
1 lb = 450 g (454 g)
1 oz = 30 g (28 g)

10 9 8 7 6 5 4 3 2 1

Published by Sterling Publishing Company, Inc.
387 Park Avenue South, New York, N.Y. 10016
Originally published by Rudra Press
under the tilte *Eating in Eden*
© 1998 by Hermine Freed
Distributed in Canada by Sterling Publishing
℅ Canadian Manda Group, One Atlantic Avenue, Suite 105
Toronto, Ontario, Canada M6K 3E7
Distributed in Great Britain and Europe by Cassell PLC
Wellington House, 125 Strand, London WC2R 0BB, England
Distributed in Australia by Capricorn Link (Australia) Pty Ltd.
P.O. Box 6651, Baulkham Hills, Business Centre, NSW 2153, Australia

Sterling ISBN 0-8069-2277-X

TABLE OF CONTENTS

Part II: Recipes

PART III: FOR YOUR REFERENCE

introduction

HERMINE'S STORY

It is now four years since I was diagnosed with breast cancer. Like so many who face cancer, I wondered, "Why me?" It was a wake-up call that forced me to look mortality in the eye. I had a rare type of the disease which tends to appear in both breasts, and my doctor wanted to perform a double mastectomy. The first thing I changed was my doctor. The new doctor agreed with the diagnosis, but suggested that a tendency was not a fact, advising me to leave the second breast alone unless cancer was found in it. But what could I do to prevent the cancer from recurring?

If I was doing something in my life to cause the cancer, this should be the first thing to change. While I knew that the causes of many cancers are unknown, I understood there was a link between diet and cancer. This was a place for me to start. At the time I began this book it was hard to find allopathic medical doctors who address cancer prevention through diet,* so I turned to alternative sources for my information.

I had read *Quantum Healing* by Deepak Chopra many years before and had remembered it as a book that logically and intelligently explains the mind-body connection. Chopra, an Indian doctor trained both in the traditional Aryuvedic practices of his native country and allopathic medicine, had successfully treated people for cancer using meditation and other alternative techniques. Barry Bryant, author of *Cancer and Consciousness*, taught me meditation

---

*Since my diagnosis, there have been positive changes in the way that the Western medical profession views prevention. Many doctors and insurance providers suggest dietary change as an aid to health care. Much research has been done on the subject of food and health, and that has contributed enormously to the empirical evidence in this book.

and provided me with his book, which addressed not only meditation, but the fundamentals of macrobiotics and other nutritional
theories.

At about the same time, several articles appeared in *The New
York Times* reporting on research in anticarcinogenic foods. An article
that appeared the week before my surgery caught my attention:
"Chemists Learn Why Vegetables in Diet Help People Avoid Cancer."
It was an exciting and promising study, and I used it as an impetus to
do more research. *Prescription for Nutritional Healing* by James and
Phyllis Balch became a source of information about the relationships
between specific ailments and the food we consume.

I began to collect health food cookbooks that were helpful for
learning food theories and methods of substituting for animal products. However, they left me cold from the point of view of the
palate. I had long been a gourmet cook, eating all manner of arcane
foods, and while I was willing to go cold turkey on animal products
and other harmful foods, I was not prepared to give up food that
tasted good. Vegetarian cookbooks offered appealing recipes, but
relied too much on eggs, dairy, and fats. Michio Kushi's books on
macrobiotics were important for learning some of the fundamentals
about food and health, but while there is much to agree with in his
thinking, there is also much to dispute. Macrobiotics was (and perhaps still is) the prevailing source of health food information, but I
felt that it was too reliant on Japanese foods, ignoring herbs as a sea-
soning, and eliminating all foods that could be potentially harmful,
no matter how unlikely the harm.

I was not getting much support from the medical profession,
which seemed to ignore both the information I received from these
sources and the almost daily reports I read in *The New York Times*.
Therefore, it was most heartening to find two books written by
M.D.s, *Food for Life* by Dr. Neal Barnard and *Save Yourself from
Breast Cancer* by Robert M. Kradjian, which stress the need for a
vegan, virtually no-fat diet.

There are topics of dispute in all these works, and it was necessary to weed through it and save the most logical ideas for my own
diet. In fact, there is contention about almost every theory related to
food. Alternative medicine relies heavily on anecdotal evidence, and
the scientific community only supports empirical proof. For example, despite many studies and reports that pesticides can be car-

cinogenic, Memorial Sloan Kettering Hospital in New York will not endorse patient consumption of organically produced foods until their own study proves (or disproves) the dangers of pesticides. This flies in the face of scientific studies that show that certain pesticides mimic estrogen in the body, and raised estrogen levels are an important factor in causing breast cancer. The FDA functions in much the same way. The danger in this is that many people will eat any food that is approved by the FDA on the assumption that the FDA would do no harm. This may not be the case.

My own diet was far less pernicious than most, but I got breast cancer. I spent my summers in the Hamptons, on the eastern end of Long Island, New York, living, usually, at the edge of a farm field. For summer after summer, I planted a vegetable garden at the edge of the field, I drank the well water, and I breathed, ate, and drank the chemicals that the farmers sprayed. My husband has Parkinson's disease, an idiopathic disorder, meaning that there is no known cause, but what many believe is exacerbated by pesticides. I am not going to wait for the FDA or Memorial Sloan Kettering to finish their studies. I simply eat organic produce now.

I have always loved cooking and am accomplished at the art of food preparation, so translating my skills to a special diet became a challenge and a pleasure. I have written this book because I want to share what I have learned. It is hard to give up old habits and relinquish the foods you love. But I truly believe that the food I eat now is more varied and interesting than before. The standard meal of meat (or poultry or fish) and two vegetables, even when exquisitely prepared, can seem dull compared to the variety of a vegan diet.

Unfortunately, most health food cookbooks and restaurants do not cater to people who love to eat. They have put a terrible onus on eating for health. Most people recoil in horror when faced with the prospect of a life of healthful eating. When I told a friend that I was writing a gourmet health food cookbook, she said "Isn't that an oxymoron?" But this need not be the case. I have written this book for everyone who wants to have a healthful diet and who also enjoys good food. The recipes are largely vegan (vegetarian, non-dairy) and are low-fat or non-fat. Eating for your health means more than giving up meat and dairy, however, since the food industry has tampered with our food products so severely. Therefore, it is important to learn about good nutrition as well as to follow the recipes.

For people with severe illnesses, I recommend consulting a nutritionist with experience in nutritional healing to address your particular problem. There might be specific dietary problems that are not addressed in this book. What nourishes one person may poison another. For example, normally I would strongly recommend the use of sesame seeds as a source of calcium, but I have a friend who is allergic to sesame. Another friend has Graves' Disease (a hyperthyroid condition). The food recommended for her hyperthyroidism—a minimum of cruciferous vegetables and plenty of eggs—is not what I would recommend myself. But nothing is for everyone. If you are healthy, this book should keep you that way. If you are not, it will *make* you healthy.

One of my great pleasures is preparing dinner for friends and receiving their compliments. When I tell them that they have just eaten health food, they tell me that if they could learn how to make such wonderful meals, they would eat health food, too. I have written this book for my friends who would like to eat well and for all of you who would be tempted to take better care of yourselves if only you knew how.

PART 1
About Food

one

THE FOOD-HEALTH CONNECTION

Many people still find it difficult to believe that disease may have its roots in dietary habits, despite the fact that vitamin-deficiency-related diseases, food allergies, and food poisoning are clearly understood in our culture. The long-term effects of a bad diet are particularly hard to comprehend as we cannot perceive their immediate results.

It seems as if whenever I discuss the subject of food and health with healthy people, they bring up their 95-year-old uncle who has had bacon and eggs every morning of his life, steak and french fries every night, never ate a salad, and has never even had a cold. I have many responses to that, but let's start with the idea that we are all shaped by a balance between nature and nurture, between our genes and how we live, and this is true whether we're talking about health or intelligence. Your uncle may have excellent genes. If you don't share his good fortune, a healthy diet can help prevent disease for which you have a genetic predisposition. My other answer to the aged-uncle question is that all foods were produced organically until the '50s, so your old relatives started their lives with healthful foods. And they lived their early lives before the environment was tainted by chemicals and nuclear fallout.

TWO TIERS OF FOOD-RELATED PROBLEMS

There are essentially two tiers of food-related problems that I categorize as short-term and long-term health problems.

Short-Term Problems

Short-term instigators are pathogens such as salmonella (which may be found in raw meat, fish, or eggs), or toxins such as aflatoxins that occur naturally in some plants. Both act instantaneously on their victims, causing gastrointestinal disorders which range from the upsetting, like nausea, to the fatal. Raw fish is sometimes infected with parasites, but these are visible to the naked eye and can be removed from the fish by cutting them away. However, it is wisest to avoid these foods if you are afraid they will make you ill. It is safest to cook foods thoroughly as heat will kill most pathogens.

Long-Term Problems

Long-term disorders are exacerbated by eating foods over a long period of time that do not appear to be doing any harm, but in fact have a cumulative effect in the body. By the time they are discovered, it is often too late. For example, foods loaded with fat and cholesterol often contain additives and pesticides and have been linked to cancer and heart disease as well as gastrointestinal and neurological disorders.

Often there are short-term warnings signaling stresses that may become long-term problems. For instance, TV commercials recommend that you take this or that antacid to relieve the indigestion caused by eating fatty, fried foods. The answer is not to take antacids, but to avoid the fatty and fried foods. The indigestion is only the tip of the iceberg. Long-term consumption of such foods can cause ulcers, diverticulitis, Crohn's disease, colitis, and colon cancer.

A healthy diet should help you remain disease-free. Your immune system will not be spending its time fighting off food toxins and will be strong enough to battle any microbes that come your way. A sound diet will provide you with all the phytochemicals (plant-derived products) necessary to keep your system in healthy balance.

two

FOODS THAT HURT

Our food supply has become so tainted—with chemicals, antibiotics, hormones, pesticides, preservatives, food additives, artificial colorings and flavorings, irradiation, overprocessed and bleached flours, rices and sugars—that it has become an act of self-defense to eat well. We are getting ill from all of this tampering with the food supply—cancer is on the rise, heart disease is on the rise, new immune deficiency diseases are surfacing yearly.

What is wrong with the traditional American diet? And what can be done to make it more wholesome? Everyone learns about the food pyramid with seeds and grains at the bottom and fats at the top. The pyramid promotes the idea that our basic diet should come from seeds and grains, to be augmented with fruits and vegetables. Meats, sweets, and fats are to be only a small part of the diet. Yet the traditional American diet is centered on meat with few fresh fruits and vegetables. Bacon, eggs, and butter are what many people start the day with—overloading the body upon waking with cholesterol and fat and providing very little fiber. These foods are so heavy that the most tempting thing to do after breakfast is nap. Perhaps that is why so many Americans overindulge in coffee, another toxic substance. The caffeine in the coffee props them up after a heavy breakfast, and keeps them jazzed until the next food attack.

THE BAD (AND POTENTIALLY BAD) FOODS

The information in the following sections is crucial to your health.

Meat and Poultry

Animals are often raised with hormones used to induce prema-
ture acceleration of growth, and with antibiotics used to ward off
diseases. When we eat meat and poultry, the entrance of these
antibiotics and hormones into our own bodies subjects us to an array
of problems. Children are especially affected by the hormones in
food. As an example, American girls reach menarche about 6 to 8
years earlier today than they did a century ago, possibly due to overconsumption of hormone-rich milk.

If hormones and antibiotics were the only problem with animal
products, eating meat from organically raised animals would be the
solution. Unfortunately, meat and poultry pose other health problems. Cholesterol exists only in animal products (meat, poultry,
dairy, eggs, and fish). Plants contain no cholesterol. Cholesterol
clogs the arteries and promotes heart disease. Animal fat is saturated fat (see "Fats") and saturated fat stimulates the production of hormones, which can speed the growth of tumors and cancer cells.

Indigestion is much more common to the meat consumer than
to the vegetarian. There is no fiber in meat, so a diet heavy on meat
and low on fresh fruits and vegetables can cause constipation, acid
stomach, diverticulitis, colon cancer, Crohn's disease, and other
digestive ailments.

Dairy

Dairy products and eggs contain the same pesticides, antibiotics, and hormones that contaminate many cows and chickens.
There are those who believe that milk is meant for baby cows, not
for humans (please note that adult cows do not drink milk), and
there are many reasons for this. Many people suffer from lactose
sensitivity and other milk allergies. Milk may exacerbate diabetes,
and there is much evidence that it actually contributes to osteoporosis rather than preventing it, as animal proteins can interfere
with calcium absorption. Skim milk is presumably more harmful in
this regard as it is higher in protein than whole milk. Ironically, then,
the dairy which is apparently necessary for obtaining calcium actually gets in the way of its absorption. Milk is also hard to digest. As
for eggs, even if they come from organically raised chickens, they are
still extremely high in cholesterol and should be avoided.

Fats

There are basically three types of fat—polyunsaturated, monounsaturated, and saturated. Saturated fats found in meats, poultry, and dairy are the most harmful. They are the source of cholesterol which can lead to arterial clogging and heart disease. Saturated fats can also feed cancers.

Most vegetable oils are high in poly- or monounsaturated fats and low in saturated fats. Polyunsaturated fats contain essential fatty acids, and some are actually necessary for the maintenance of good health. A new study has suggested that polyunsaturated fats, found in corn, safflower, sunflower, and soybean oils, can reduce bad cholesterol and lower the risk of coronary heart disease.

"Trans" fats are produced when vegetable oils are hydrogenated to make them solid. Margarine, most soy cream cheeses (except those in health food stores), and shortening are hydrogenated and high in trans fats, posing the same dangers as saturated fats derived from animal sources. Most margarines are a poor choice not only because of the fat, but also because they contain more chemicals than natural ingredients.

It is hard to have a 100% fat-free diet. Even vegetables contain small amounts, and this amount is necessary for the body.

Oils

There are many differences of opinion about oils. Some suggest that monounsaturated fats, found in olive oil, canola oil, and sesame oil, are the most beneficial. While some oils are beneficial, none should be consumed in high quantities. Very little fat is necessary to the body, and the harm of overconsumption is far-reaching. It can interfere with absorption of other nutrients. Calcium intake, for example, is impeded by fats, so that those on a low-fat diet actually require less calcium. Even vegetable fats can be carcinogenic if overconsumed. Cancerous tumors bind to fats, so it's believed that a low-fat diet can starve tumors.

For the purpose of taste, I suggest using olive oil for most Western cooking, especially Italian dishes, and canola and sesame oil for most Asian cooking. Canola oil should be used when you don't want the flavor of the oil to distract from the taste of the ingredients. Corn, safflower, or canola oil can be used in baking. Sesame oil adds a strong, distinctive flavor of its own. Coconut and palm oils are the only vegetable oils that are high in saturated fats and should be avoided.

Most commercial oils are highly processed with chemicals and bleaches used to "refine" them. They are heated to the point where they lose most of their valuable vitamin E. Cold-pressed oils are produced in the most natural way, expelling the oil safely, and are the only oils that should be used. Except for olive oil, cold-pressed oils are hard to find outside the health food industry.

Flour

To make white flour the husk is removed from the wheat, taking away vital nutrients, and then it is bleached. Bleaching is done with chlorine, a known carcinogen. When you eat foods made with bleached flour you are eating empty calories. "Enriched" flour has vitamins and minerals added back to it after they have been removed by milling. It is like paste with a vitamin pill stuck in it. When I specify flour in a recipe in this book, I mean unbleached flour, and usually whole wheat. The unbleached white flour does have the husk removed, so it is lower in nutrients than whole flour. But there is no chlorine in it to do harm, and there are still nutrients left in the core. For those with a wheat intolerance, other flours such as amaranth, spelt, or quinoa (a high-protein grain from the Andes) can be substituted.

Salt

Salt is another overly processed food product. Table salt has no nutrients, is bleached, and is high in sodium. Sea salt, as unrefined as possible, is full of natural minerals that are good for you. Many sea salts are processed and the minerals are removed. Use an unrefined sea salt and if you have special salt-related health problems, such as high blood pressure, try to avoid salt altogether. You'll get used to unsalted foods after a while and will probably find you like no salt better than a substitute.

Sugar

Most of our sugar, which isn't the best thing to eat even in its purest state, is also bleached and leached of nutrients. Some people eat a candy bar to get quick energy. How does that work? Sugars enter the bloodstream quickly, and a sudden rise in blood sugar releases insulin, which gives a jolt of energy. That may work in the short run, but if sugar is consumed often it can result in an insulin imbalance. That, in turn, can lead to a variety of disorders from diabetes to hypoglycemia to nutrient imbalances. What is more, insulin is the hunger hormone. The more of it there is in the blood, the more likely you are to feel hungry. There are some people who believe that the food producers purposely overload food with sugar to induce you to eat more. Many nutritionists think that sugar is worse than meat as it promotes certain food allergies and interferes with the body's metabolism.

Sucanat is evaporated, ground sugarcane juice, unprocessed and unbleached. It can be used in place of white sugar in small amounts. Maple syrup and barley syrup are also healthier substitutes. The natural sweeteners in fruits are usually all you need. Sugar that is sold as "raw sugar" (or turbinado sugar) is actually not raw sugar at all, but sucrose, which is bleached sugar to which molasses has been added. Impurities may have been removed, but so have the nutrients. Brown sugar is similar. You may be tempted to use fructose as a substitute, as it is naturally found in fruit. However, it seems to do as much, if not more, harm to the body as ordinary sucrose, which is the most common commercially available sugar. *Do not* use Equal[tm], Sweet'N Low[tm], aspartame, or other such products, which are pure chemicals and worse for you than sugar.

Fish

Fish oils (such as omega-3 fatty acids) are only found in fish and flaxseed, and are actually beneficial because they contain certain nutrients, like vitamin B12, which are not found in vegetables. But due to the fact that much of our water supply is polluted, with polychlorinated biphenyls (PCBs), mercury, and chemical run-offs from farm fields and industrial plants, there can be more of a chemical threat eating fish than eating non-organic vegetables. Some fish are better for you than others: flounder, sole, cod, and salmon are the best for you. Swordfish is very fatty. Shellfish should be avoided because they are bottom-feeders and pick up the worst of the pollutants. Lobster and shrimp are high in cholesterol.

THE BAD THINGS WE DO TO FOODS

The information that follows should be required reading for everyone concerned about the quality of the food they eat.

Pesticides

Chemicals and pesticides have increased crop yield and provided more food for more people, but they have also depleted our soil, which has resulted in nutrient-poor foods filled with carcinogenic chemicals. Many pesticides mimic estrogen in the body, which means that they induce or exacerbate certain cancers, especially breast, ovarian, and prostate cancers. Pesticides are particularly pernicious for children who eat non-organic foods and are often overloaded by the time they are five. There are neurotoxins in many pesticides that are thought to be safe for adults, but have been linked to brain damage in children.

The foods that absorb and retain the most pesticides, and that should therefore be eaten only in their organic state, are apples, carrots, grapes, green beans, lettuce, oranges, peaches, peanuts, potatoes, strawberries, and wheat.

Irradiated Foods

Although irradiation has been tested as a method of preserving produce, it has only been implemented in recent years. Fruits and vegetables are irradiated, apparently with the waste materials from nuclear power production, to kill all bacteria, mold, and fungus that could grow on them. It is a very effective method of keeping the produce fresh through long journeys, even preserving its vitamins. However, the produce is still irradiated when you eat it. The FDA says it's safe, but irradiation hasn't been available long enough to test long-term results. There is evidence that irradiated foods have caused chromosomal damage, released free radicals (which are, in high amounts, considered to be cancer precursors), and raised toxicity levels in the body. The real problem is that foods are not identified as being irradiated, which means that the more beautiful a pile of apples looks, the more you may have to be suspicious that it is irradiated. Organic produce is never irradiated, so once again, you are safer buying your food at a health food store.

The irradiation of meat has just been approved to kill bacteria which cause food poisoning. When the meat is irradiated at the packing plant, it kills all the bacteria, both harmful and harmless. As that meat goes from the point of irradiation to the wholesaler to the butcher shop, it can pick up new bacteria. These new bacteria may grow more rapidly than the original ones because they no longer have to compete with the harmless bacteria.

Processed Foods

Reading labels on foods in the freezer department can be quite an eye opener. Try it. Many of them are so full of chemicals and additives that it is a wonder they provide any nutrition at all. Some of these chemicals, such as nitrates, MSG, and saccharin, are tumor-initiators. Hot dogs and other processed meats that are made with nitrates are carcinogenic. When you buy prepared foods, be careful to read labels, even in health food stores, and stay away from chemicals and additives. Be sure there are no added sugars or bleached flours, and check the fat content. Be careful about eggs, butter, and hydrogenated fats and oils. Try to buy products made with organic produce.

Wax and Petroleum Coatings

Most supermarket produce is covered with wax or petroleum— not just the cucumbers, but virtually everything, including the lettuce. This is done to preserve the food in shipment and to make it look good. It is better for food to look awful and be good than to have it be awful and look good. You can peel the cucumbers, but not the lettuce. You can wash, but I doubt that you'll remove it all. This is another good reason for buying food from farm stands, urban farmers' markets, and organic markets rather than from supermarkets.

three

FOODS THAT HELP

To counteract the negative news, there is just as much good news. In the last few years, a great deal of research has been done on the relationship between food and health. Many foods are anticarcinogenic and there are those that can boost the immune system. There are also foods that are "heart smart." This should hardly seem strange, as, after all, herbalists have cured diseases with foods for thousands of years, and vitamin-deficiency diseases are cured by eating the right foods. The very foods that we consume daily can be as potent as exotic herbs from distant rain forests.

ORGANICALLY GROWN PRODUCE

Happily, there are farms that grow their produce organically, using natural fertilizers like fish emulsion, seaweed, and compost and natural pesticides like bugs. The natural fertilizers give the foods nutrients that chemical fertilizers cannot provide, and both growing and shipping methods have improved so much that organics generally look better (and certainly taste better) than non-organic foods. In some cases, it is the farmers' own experiences with pesticides that have converted them to organic methods. The Green Thumb is an organic farm and market in Watermill, New York. The owners, the Halseys, come from a large farm family that has been in the region for many generations, and are the only branch of the family whose farm is organic. Johanna Halsey said that the inspiration came from her father. He was out spraying the fields one day and got one drop of pesticide in a cut in his finger. An hour later he lay paralyzed in the hospital. Mr. Halsey pulled through. But the family realized that if one drop of pesticide could do that much damage, it must do terrible harm to the body when ingested day after day. So they slowly learned organic farming and converted their farm.

I visited one day when the New York state organic inspector was there, and was very impressed with the extent to which he inspected the farm to give it certification. The ground had to be free of chemical fertilizers and pesticides, and had to be farmed organically for at least eight years. The nutritional content of the soil was inspected, as were the nutrients put into the soil. Pest control was inspected. The produce itself was inspected. For those of you who worry that organic is just a tag stuck onto a label, rest assured. I learned that day that it is a very meaningful label.

More and more great restaurants are using organic produce, not only because it is better for our health, but because it tastes better. Hopefully, as it becomes a major public health issue, we will see more and more farms convert. Not only do the foods do more good for your body, but getting the pesticides out of our air and out of our ground water will keep us healthier, too.

Most cities have organic markets. If you do not shop in those markets, or if none exist in your town, I recommend that you ask your local markets to supply you with organic foods.

I will not specify, in each recipe, that you use organic products. Instead, I am saying here that you ought to use organic foods in your cooking. If one ingredient is not organic, it is hardly as bad as if none of them are. But, you should know where your food comes from and you should know which fruits and vegetables are most likely to be heavily sprayed. One further caution: There are certain pesticides which are banned in the U.S. However, they are used in other countries. This means that a lot of food we eat in winter may have been sprayed with the very pesticides we do not permit here, because we've imported the food from South America where pesticides are used. Often, farmers obtain the pesticides abroad and use them here despite the ban.

Unless impossible to find in any other form, fruits and vegetables should be fresh, not frozen or canned. Not only is the taste of food directly related to the quality of the ingredients, but the fresher the food, the better it is for you. Nutrients dissipate as produce ages.

ANTIOXIDANTS AND PHYTOCHEMICALS

Antioxidants are important in the diet, particularly as cancer fighting agents. What are they and what do they do? Simply put, they sop up free radicals, which are unstable molecules (they have unpaired electrons that are always looking for another molecule to complete the pair). The instability of these free radicals can lead to a chain reaction which leads to fast-growing cancer cells. In the body, free radicals can mutate cells, harm enzymes and proteins, and damage cells. Where do these free radicals come from? They can be created by external forces, such as chemical pollutants, chemical additives to foods, radiation, cigarettes, and viruses, but can also be triggered by faulty genes and hormones. Antioxidants and phytochemicals (chemical nutrients found in foods) can destroy free radicals before they do their harm.

Under normal conditions, most of us probably have cancer cells in our body. When we are healthy, they are attacked by the body's antioxidant enzymes and they do us no harm. It is only when our systems go out of balance for a variety of reasons (some listed above) that the cancer takes over. Sometimes the imbalance comes from a poor diet. A diet rich in antioxidants, found in fruits and vegetables, is crucial to the healthy balance of the body, and can help fight cancer cells before they become tumors. Some phytochemicals destroy blood vessels that feed carcinogenic tumors, making it harder for them to grow. If you have, or have had cancer, it is crucial that you change your eating habits to include many antioxidant-rich fruits and vegetables.

Among the most potent cancer-fighters are carotenes, flavonoids, indoles, and monoterpenes. They are found in carrots, squash, tomatoes, red and yellow peppers, citrus fruits, cantaloupes, and other yellow-orange fruits and vegetables, as well as leafy greens like spinach, cabbage, broccoli, chard, and kale. See the chart at the end of the book for a list of important nutrients along with the names and sources of a variety of antioxidants and phytochemicals.

FIBER

The discussion of fiber is probably familiar to you as it has received considerable media coverage, particularly as a laxative.

Most grains, fruits, and vegetables contain some fiber. Meat products have none at all. Fiber acts like a sponge in the colon, sopping up carcinogens and moving waste through the system faster by nurturing good bacteria and yeasts and detoxifying chemicals. This helps fight cancer and gives fiber its power as a laxative. Vegetarians generally suffer less constipation than their meat-eating counterparts.

Because the fiber level in whole wheat is considerably higher than in refined wheat, you are far better off eating whole wheat bread and other whole grains. Bleached flours provide empty calories without the benefit of fiber. Fiber helps keep a healthy balance of intestinal flora, and it fights cholesterol, helping the cardiovascular system as well as fighting cancer. There are two kinds of fiber, soluble and insoluble. Soluble fiber is found in bran, especially oat bran. Insoluble fiber consists of pectins, gums, and mucilages. It is found in fruits and vegetables and helps with sugar metabolism and the prevention of diabetes.

IMMUNE SYSTEM BOOSTERS

Garlic and onions contain allylic sulfides that both fight cancers and help the immune system. Garlic is one of the best medicines you can find. In addition to the above mentioned benefits, it also lowers cholesterol, regulates blood pressure, keeps the heart healthy and may help fight rheumatism. It is at its best raw, as many of its healing nutrients are depleted in cooking. Recipes are supplied which include both the raw and the cooked. Don't worry about garlic breath. Normal consumption doesn't cause it. Generally, garlic odor is associated with indigestion. Also, using parsley with garlic cuts the smell. All allium plants—onions, leeks, garlic, scallions, shallots, and chives—contain a variety of organosulfides that help block the growth of tumors (particularly in the stomach, colon, and breast), boost the immune system and help the digestive tract. Many of my recipes contain garlic and onions—both for your health and for your palate. Not only are they good for you, but they add flavor to food.

Substances that boost immunity are manganese, zinc, coenzyme Q10, selenium, flavonoids, lentinan (found in shitake mushrooms only), beta-carotene, vitamins A, C, and E, and thiols.

These immune system boosters can keep the body in healthy balance and help fight off disease.

SOY

Soybean products are thought to protect against cancer as well. Amongst other virtues, soybeans contain genistein. Genistein blocks growth of new blood vessels that harbor the growth of tumors and prevent growth of cancer cells. Japanese people who eat a traditional diet, which includes soy products, have far less cancer than those who eat a Western-style diet. The Japanese diet is low in meat and dairy and rich in lightly cooked vegetables and tofu. For several years, tofu has been praised for its ability to ward off breast and prostate cancer and to help fight post-menopausal symptoms. Now there are new reports suggesting that soy protein lowers bad cholesterol, while not affecting the good. Soy is really rather miraculous. It is a little bean which can transform itself into all sorts of forms: soy sauce, soy milk, tofu, soy hot dogs and burgers, tempeh, and cheeses.

VITAMINS

Finally, we all know that vitamins are good for you. They do everything from regulate the organ systems, to enrich the blood and boost the immune system. A complete list of vitamins and their functions is presented at the end of the book.

four

A VEGAN DIET: HURT OR HELP?

There are many people who worry that a vegan diet will deprive them of necessary nutrients supposedly found only in animal products. In fact, usually dietary and nutritional needs are best met through a vegan diet. Common concerns are addressed below.

CALCIUM INTAKE

Probably the biggest fear about giving up dairy is the loss of calcium in the diet. However, there are many foods whose calcium levels surpass that of milk or that allow the body to process calcium more efficiently. Sesame seeds are rich in calcium as are seaweed products. Green, leafy, and cruciferous vegetables such as chard and broccoli (the darker the green, the more calcium), and beans are also rich in calcium. As mentioned above, a diet free of animal proteins makes better use of calcium than one which relies on dairy for calcium. The interaction of calcium with animal protein actually lowers the amount of calcium absorbed by the body. Therefore, the calcium that you get from vegetable sources is actually used more efficiently by the body than the calcium in milk. Check the daily calcium you are getting from the nutrition information given with each recipe in this book. If you are deficient for the day, it is a good idea to take a supplement. Beware of drinking sodas if your calcium level concerns you. The phosphorus in soda depletes calcium. To avoid osteoporosis, the softening of the bones caused by depleted calcium, it is also a good idea to do some exercise every day. Walking briskly for about a mile is very beneficial.

PROTEIN LEVELS

Non-vegetarians worry more about the lack of protein than anything else. However, there is evidence that most Westerners overload
themselves on protein. The lack of protein does not cause a lack in
energy. Protein is a cell-building material, not an energy source.
Remember that marathon runners stock up on pasta before a run.
Carbohydrates—not protein—are the energy source.

While it is true that plant proteins are not complete amino acids,
a mix of grains and legumes will make up the deficit. Past health
food methods (used by many health food restaurants and cookbooks) include mixing beans and rice, a sure-fire way to get a complete protein. While this method works, it is also unnecessary. If you
eat a balanced diet of grains, legumes, fresh vegetables and fruits,
and nuts and seeds, you will, over the course of time, stay in balance. Often, you will eat beans and rice without even thinking about
it if you use soy products (derived from soy beans) like tofu. A meal
of stir-fried vegetables and tofu with brown rice is a meal of beans
and rice.

SOURCES OF IRON

When we think of iron, most of us think of liver and red meat.
However, there are many vegetarian sources of iron. Much higher
levels of iron are found in seaweed (particularly hijiki), and nuts
than are found in meat, and most dried beans, like white beans,
chickpeas, and black beans are iron-rich. Certain green, leafy vegetables and parsley are a good source of iron, and a well-balanced
vegetarian diet should not cause an iron deficiency. A little parsley
and hijiki sprinkled on salad each day should keep you well-supplied
with iron and calcium.

SOURCES OF VITAMIN B12

Vegetarian sources of B12 include spirulina, sea vegetables,
miso, and tempeh. However, these sources of B12 are inactive
derivatives rather than the active vitamin. Therefore, you would do
well to take a B12 supplement two or three times a week. Because
vitamin B12 requirements are small and it is both stored and recy-
cled in the body, symptoms of deficiency may be delayed for years.

Absorption of B12 becomes less efficient as the body ages, so supplements may be advised for older vegetarians.

Many recipes in this book call for tofu. Except for the recipes for sauces and dressings, you could substitute tempeh. You might also consider using miso instead of salt in your cooking to get additional B12.

SOURCES OF VITAMIN E

Those marvelous green leafy vegetables are a great source of vitamin E. Other sources are nuts, oils, and grains. Megadoses of vitamin E, a strong antioxidant, are recommended for certain health problems, and the only way to fulfill that need, vegan or not, is with supplements. Large doses are suggested to alleviate some symptoms of menopause, and its antioxidant properties are good for fighting cancer and Parkinson's disease.

SOURCES OF OMEGA-3 FATTY ACIDS

Fatty acids are mostly found in fish. You should be aware of two important vegetable sources. Flaxseed is one; it is best used as a supplement, as there is little one can do with it in cooking. Purslane is the other. Anyone who grows a vegetable garden knows purslane as a small, fat-leafed weed that often gets weeded right out of your garden. If you find it, add it to your mesclun mix, or just sprinkle some into your salad.

PART II
Recipes

APPETIZERS AND PATÉS

MUSHROOM TARTS

One great difficulty in a vegan diet is preparing baked goods. Pie crusts are at their best when made with butter, and lots of it, but that is not permitted here. Margarine is no substitute and oil is still fat. In this case, the solution is to use phyllo dough. It makes a light, delicious tart.

Use a variety of mushrooms—whatever is available in your market. White mushrooms are the most available and cheapest, though not the most nutritious. Portabellos are a bit heavy for this dish. Shitake mushrooms are healthful and considered great cancer fighters. They are antiviral and lower blood pressure and cholesterol. Reishi mushrooms, a variety of shitake, are quite medicinal. Many wild mushrooms are poisonous, so unless you are an expert, stick to what is in the market.

6 shitake mushrooms
1/2 cup chopped leeks or scallions
1 teaspoon olive oil
1/2 lb. white mushrooms, chopped, or a variety of mushrooms
5 cloves garlic, minced
3 tablespoons chopped tarragon
2 tablespoons chopped parsley
3 tablespoons vegetable stock
3 tablespoons casein-free soy parmesan
4 large sheets of phyllo
olive oil to brush phyllo

Soak the shitakes in water until soft (or use fresh shitakes). Remove and discard the stems and chop. Sauté the leeks in olive oil and add the shitakes, mushrooms, and garlic. Stir until soft. Add the herbs, reserving 1 tablespoon of the tarragon, and the stock and stir until liquid is absorbed. Add the soy parmesan.

continued

Most packaged phyllo is made from bleached flour and may have chemical preservatives. If you can't find any that suits you, my recipe is on pages 138-139.

Take a large sheet of phyllo and brush lightly with olive oil. Fold over twice. Leave one layer open and turn the phyllo into a circle. It should be shaped like a cup. Repeat with the other pieces. Bake for about 5 minutes in a 350° oven. Fill each with mushroom mixture and bake for 10 minutes more. Sprinkle the tops with tarragon.

Variation: Mushroom turnovers. Fold phyllo in half and brush with olive oil. Put 3 tablespoons of the mushroom mixture on one side of it. Fold the sides over and roll, keeping it flat. Bake in a 350° oven for 20 minutes. Serve plain or with a roasted red pepper vinaigrette (page 64).

Serves 4

Nutritional analysis per serving: 138 calories; 3.5 g fat (21.6% calories from fat); 0 mg cholesterol; 22.3 g carbohydrate; 6.4 g protein; 272 mg sodium; 587 mg calcium; 2.6 mg iron; 7 mg vitamin C

❀❀

STUFFED MUSHROOMS

Any mushroom is suitable as long as it has a bowl-like cap to hold the stuffing. In this recipe, cremini would be best.

1 lb. cremini mushrooms
4 shallots, chopped
1 tablespoon olive oil
4 cloves garlic, minced
3/4 cups bread crumbs, preferably made from stale bread
1 tablespoon chopped basil
1 tablespoon chopped parsley
1 tablespoon chopped oregano or marjoram
1/4 cup casein-free soy parmesan
pinch of ground nutmeg
sea salt and pepper to taste

Remove the stems from the mushrooms and chop. Chop the shallots and sauté in olive oil until they just turn soft and brown. Add the garlic and mushroom stems and cook, stirring, until the mushrooms wilt. Add herbs and bread crumbs and sprinkle with a few tablespoons of water. Turn off the heat and add soy parmesan and seasonings. Fill the mushroom caps with the mixture and place in a non-stick baking pan (or brush oil on a regular pan) and bake until mushrooms are cooked through (about 15 minutes).

Serves 4 to 6

Nutritional analysis per serving: 137 calories; 4.9 g fat (30.5% calories from fat); 0 mg cholesterol; 18.6 g carbohydrate; 6.4 g protein; 246 mg sodium; 637 mg calcium; 2.6 mg iron; 5 mg vitamin C

CHILLED SHITAKE MUSHROOMS

The health benefits of shitake mushrooms make this dish a delicious preventive medicine.

20 shitake mushrooms
1/2 cup stock made with the mushroom water
1 tablespoon sucanat
2 tablespoons soy sauce
1 teaspoon sesame oil

Soak the mushrooms in water until soft. Use the mushroom water to make a stock (page 83), then put the stock in a pan and bring to a boil. Reduce the heat and add the mushrooms. Cook for about 10 minutes and add the sucanat and soy sauce. Continue cooking a few minutes more. Remove from the heat and chill. When cool, slice the mushrooms and sprinkle with sesame oil. Arrange in a circle on a plate and serve. Serve with chilled cucumbers.

Serves 4 to 8

Nutritional analysis per serving: 66 calories; 1.2 g fat (15.3% calories from fat); 0 mg cholesterol; 13.3 g carbohydrate;1.9 g protein; 487 mg sodium; 5 mg calcium; 0.5 mg iron; 1 mg vitamin C

CHILLED CUCUMBERS WITH
SESAME DRESSING

These can be served along with the chilled shitake mushrooms, either on the same plate or as a nibble before dinner.

1 large or 3 kirby cucumbers
2 tablespoons soy sauce
1 teaspoon sesame oil
1 tablespoon sesame seeds

Cut the cucumbers in half lengthwise, then into 1/8-inch slices. Put on a plate and cover them with the soy sauce, sesame oil, and sesame seeds. Chill. These can be served with chilled shitake mushrooms.

Serves 2 to 3

Nutritional analysis per serving: 131 calories; 5.3 g fat (32.6% calories from fat); 0 mg cholesterol; 18.7 g carbohydrate; 5.7 g protein; 1041 mg sodium; 129 mg calcium; 2.5 mg iron; 31 mg vitamin C

COLD SESAME NOODLES

This is a variation on the Chinese restaurant standard. I am told it is a great dish to make for children. Those children I surveyed listed sesame noodles amongst their favorite dishes. Ditto for adults.

1 lb. udon or soba noodles
3 tablespoons tahini
3 cloves garlic, minced
2 teaspoons ginger, minced
2 tablespoons soy sauce
1/2 teaspoon chili powder
1 teaspoon sucanat
1 tablespoon sesame seeds
3 scallions, chopped
1/4 lb. snow peas
2 tablespoons chopped coriander (optional)

Cook the noodles in a pot of boiling water and cool. Mix all the other ingredients except the scallions, snow peas, and coriander in a bowl. If too thick, add a little water. Add the cooked noodles and toss until they are well coated. Arrange several snow peas on the edge of each plate and place the noodles at the center. Sprinkle the top with scallions and coriander.

Serves 4

Nutritional analysis per serving: 505 calories; 9.4 g fat (15.5% calories from fat); 0 mg cholesterol; 93.6 g carbohydrate; 20.7 g protein; 1490 mg sodium; 203 mg calcium; 6.8 mg iron; 16 mg vitamin C

VIETNAMESE SPRING ROLLS

Most Asian countries have some version of a spring roll, and most are deep-fried. This one, sometimes called a summer roll, is mostly raw, a salad wrapped in rice paper. Several ingredients in this dish may be difficult to find in a health food store or a supermarket. The rice papers, bean threads, tree ears, water chestnuts, bean sprouts, and shitake mushrooms can be purchased at an Asian market.

8 rice papers	1 medium carrot, shredded
8 leaves lettuce	1/4 lb. tofu in julienne slices
(Boston, red leaf, etc.)	sprig of mint
1 oz. bean thread noodles	sprig of coriander
2 medium tree ears,	1/4 cup ground peanuts
soaked in water	2 scallions, julienned
4 large shitake mushrooms,	1/4 lb. bean sprouts
soaked in water	8 water chestnuts, sliced

The rice papers come in dry sheets and should be moistened with water using a pastry brush. Brush one side, then the other—you may have to do this twice before they get soft enough to use. When thoroughly soft, place a small piece of lettuce leaf on one side of each paper. Divide the rest of the ingredients into 8 parts and place one part on on top of each paper. Fold the sides of the paper over, then roll tightly. The edges should stick together. Cover with a damp dish towel until ready to serve. Serve with peanut sauce. (See page 78.)

Makes 8 rolls

Nutritional analysis per serving: 148 calories; 3.3 g fat (19.9% calories from fat); 0 mg cholesterol; 25.4 g carbohydrate; 5.0 g protein; 75 mg sodium; 37 mg calcium; 1.5 mg iron; 6 mg vitamin C

CARROT PATÉ

This paté is rich in beta-carotene. Keep some on hand as a butter substitute.

1 medium onion, chopped
3 cloves garlic, chopped
1 teaspoon olive oil
2 cups sliced carrots
1/2 cup water
1 bay leaf
3 tablespoons chopped dill
1 tablespoon arrowroot dissolved in 1 tablespoon water
1 tablespoon agar flakes
2 tablespoons miso dissolved in 2 tablespoons water (optional)
1/4 teaspoon nutmeg, ground
1/2 cup finely chopped walnuts (optional)

Sauté the onions and garlic in olive oil until soft. Add the carrots and stir for another minute. Add the water and bay leaf and cook until the carrots are tender, about 10 minutes. Remove the bay leaf and add the dill. Purée and return to the pan. Add the arrowroot, agar, nutmeg, and (optionally) the miso and walnuts. Stir until thickened. Put in a mold and refrigerate until set. To use as a spread, eliminate the agar and put in a bowl.

Serves 6 to 8

Nutritional analysis per serving: 53 calories; 2.1 g fat (32.9% calories from fat); 0 mg cholesterol; 7.7 g carbohydrate; 1.8 g protein; 169 mg sodium; 40 mg calcium; 1.1 mg iron; 4 mg vitamin C

LENTIL PATÉ

This paté could replace a meat loaf. The curried version has an Indian flavor.

1 cup lentils
1 sprig thyme, chopped
1 bay leaf
1 medium onion, chopped
4 cloves garlic chopped
1 teaspoon olive oil
2 carrots, chopped

3 tablespoons chopped parsley
2 tablespoons chopped oregano
2 tablespoons arrowroot, dissolved
  in 1 tablespoon water
2 tablespoons agar flakes (optional)
1 teaspoon sea salt

Cook the lentils in water with the salt, parsley, bay leaf, and thyme until the lentils are soft and the water absorbed, about 20 minutes. Meanwhile, sauté the onions and garlic in olive oil for a few minutes until soft. Add the carrots and stir for a few minutes. Add to the lentils and cook another 10 minutes. Put all ingredients into a food processor, purée, and return to the pan. Mix the arrowroot in cold water and add to the mixture with the parsley and oregano. Stir until thickened.

Place in a non-stick bread pan or a lightly oiled pan, cover with aluminum foil and bake in a 350° oven for about 30 minutes. For a more delicate paté, use 2 tablespoons of agar flakes and do not bake. Put the mixture in a bread pan or another mold and refrigerate until set. Unmold and serve. To use as a spread, eliminate the agar flakes and do not bake, but cool the mixture after it has been cooked on the stove.

Serves 6 to 8

Nutritional analysis per serving: 116 calories; 1.0 g fat (7.7% calories from fat); 0 mg cholesterol; 20.7 g carbohydrate;7.5 g protein; 10 mg sodium; 57 mg calcium; 3.7 mg iron; 7 mg vitamin C

SPINACH PATÉ

Spinach is on the top ten list of foods that heal, so any excuse for another recipe is a good one. There is a Persian dish, called a coucou, which essentially is a dense quiche often made with spinach. This is a good alternative.

> 2 leeks, chopped (about 1/2 cup)
> 5 cloves garlic, chopped
> 1 teaspoon olive oil
> 1 lb. spinach, washed
> 1 lb. tofu, mashed
> 2 tablespoons chopped dill
> 1 tablespoon chopped rosemary
> 1/2 teaspoon ground nutmeg
> 1/2 cup fat-free soy milk
> 2 tablespoons arrowroot, dissolved in 2 tablespoons water
> 1 tablespoon agar flakes

Sauté the leeks and garlic in olive oil. Steam the spinach until just wilted, a minute or two. Put it in a pan with the leeks and garlic and add the tofu, dill, rosemary, and nutmeg. Stir all the ingredients together, purée, then return to pan. Add the soy milk and arrowroot and stir until thickened. Add the agar flakes. Put all the ingredients into a non-stick or lightly oiled loaf pan, cover with aluminum foil, and bake for about 45 minutes in a 350° oven, or until firm throughout.

> Serves 6 to 8

Nutritional analysis per serving: 113 calories; 4.8 g fat (35.1% calories from fat); 0 mg cholesterol; 11.5 g carbohydrate; 8.6 g protein; 55 mg sodium; 185 mg calcium; 6.7 mg iron; 19 mg vitamin C

MUSHROOM PATÉ

This makes a wonderful meat substitute, and if you eliminate the baking stage, it is a marvelous spread.

4 shallots, chopped
4 cloves garlic, chopped
1 teaspoon olive oil
1 lb. mushrooms, chopped
1/2 cup bread crumbs, soaked in water and squeezed out
1/4 teaspoon ground nutmeg
3 tablespoons chopped tarragon
2 tablespoons arrowroot or egg substitute dissolved in 2
    tablespoons water
salt and pepper to taste

Sauté the shallots and garlic in olive oil until soft. Add the mushrooms and cook until just getting soft. Add the bread crumbs and seasonings and mix well. Purée and return to the pan. Add the arrowroot or egg substitute and stir until thickened. Put all the ingredients in an oiled bread pan, cover with aluminum foil, and bake in a 350° oven for about 30 minutes.

Serves 6 to 8

Nutritional analysis per serving: 92 calories; 1.9 g fat (17.2% calories from fat); 0 mg cholesterol; 16.7 g carbohydrate; 3.6 g protein; 84 mg sodium; 61 mg calcium; 2.5mg iron; 4 mg vitamin C

SALADS

AVOCADO, GRAPEFRUIT, AND LETTUCE SALAD WITH CITRUS DRESSING

This beautiful salad is not only delicious, but rich in beta-carotene and vitamin C, too. Avocados are high in fat for a vegetable, so we should not eat them frequently; however, they are sufficiently nutritious to eat on occasion.

1 small head red or green leaf lettuce, or 2 cups mesclun mix
1 avocado, sliced
1 grapefruit opened into sections

CITRUS DRESSING:
3 tablespoons orange juice
3 tablespoons lime juice
1-inch piece of ginger, minced
2 tablespoons maple syrup
1 tablespoon olive oil
1 tablespoon chopped parsley or coriander
2 cloves minced garlic (optional)

Cover a salad plate with lettuce leaves. Make a fan of avocado slices over the lettuce on one side of the plate and one of grapefruit slices on the other. Combine the dressing ingredients and pour over the salad.

Serves 2

Nutritional analysis per serving: 302 calories; 18.6 g fat (51.6% calories from fat); 0 mg cholesterol; 36.1 g carbohydrate; 3.2 g protein; 13 mg sodium; 61 mg calcium; 1.7 mg iron; 74 mg vitamin C

BEET AND ENDIVE SALAD WITH WALNUTS

Like any vegetable, beets lose nutrients when boiled, so it is better to steam or roast them.

4 medium beets
4 endives
3 tablespoons raspberry vinegar
1 teaspoon olive oil
3 tablespoons fat-free soy milk
2 cloves garlic, minced very fine (you can use a garlic press)
2 tablespoons chopped walnuts

Steam the beets in a steamer with just enough water to last the 20 minutes it will take to cook them. Keep the skin on and leave them whole to avoid losing nutrients. Or, put them in a pan with a little water and roast them for about 30 minutes at 350°. When done, cool and cut them into 1-inch cubes. Meanwhile, cut the endives into 1-inch slices. Put one cut beet in the center of each salad plate and surround with the cut endive. Mix the oil, vinegar, and soy milk with the garlic and pour over each salad. Sprinkle with walnuts and serve.

Serves 2 to 4

Nutritional analysis per serving: 174 calories; 2.1 g fat (9.6% calories from fat); 0 mg cholesterol; 35.0 g carbohydrate; 10.1 g protein; 233 mg sodium; 338 mg calcium; 6.1 mg iron; 46 mg vitamin C

BLACK BEAN SALAD WITH PEPPERS, CORN, AND CILANTRO

This Southwestern recipe offers an exquisite mix of flavors and textures that blend together magically. The combination of beans and corn makes it a good source of protein.

1/2 cup black beans, soaked overnight
1 large red pepper
2 ears fresh corn
1 tablespoon olive oil
juice of 1 lemon
1 bunch chopped fresh cilantro
pinch of cayenne
sea salt to taste

Cook the beans in fresh water until soft. Grill the red pepper, checking it every few minutes and turning it until all its sides are charred. When cool, peel, remove the ribs and seeds, and cut into 1-inch squares. Save the juice for the sauce. Put the corn in a pot of boiling water for 1 minute. Remove with a slotted spoon and cut the kernels off the cob. Put all the ingredients in a bowl and toss.

Serves 2 to 4

Nutritional analysis per serving: 197 calories; 5.5 g fat (23.7% calories from fat); 0 mg cholesterol; 31.2 g carbohydrate; 8.9 g protein; 12 mg sodium; 74 mg calcium; 3.0 mg iron; 72 mg vitamin C

CAESAR SALAD

This is the standard Caesar salad, but without dairy or anchovies. The original is made with lightly cooked egg, still too raw to be safe, and parmesan cheese. This version eliminates the egg and substitutes soy parmesan. Also, these croutons are toasted, not fried. Worcestershire sauce is a regular ingredient, but it contains anchovy or sardine as well as molasses, so I have substituted soy sauce.

> *3 slices fresh bread (or 6 of baguette)*
> *3 cloves garlic, minced*
> *1 tablespoon Dijon mustard*
> *1 tablespoon fat-free soy milk*
> *juice of 1/2 lemon*
> *pinch of cayenne*
> *1 teaspoon soy sauce (optional)*
> *1 head Romaine lettuce*
> *2 tablespoons casein-free soy parmesan*

Cut the bread into 1-inch slices and toast, then cut it into 1-inch cubes and set aside. In a bowl mix the garlic and mustard. Add the soy milk and mix until smooth. Add the lemon juice and mix again. Add the (optional) soy sauce and cayenne. Wash and dry lettuce and add to the bowl, then add the soy parmesan and croutons, and toss.

> *Serves 2 to 4*

Nutritional analysis per serving: 68 calories; 1.3 g fat (15.4% calories from fat); 0 mg cholesterol; 10.0 g carbohydrate; 5.8 g protein; 302 mg sodium; 559 mg calcium; 2.2mg iron; 46 mg vitamin C

COLESLAW

This old standby is something you might not expect to find in a gourmet cookbook. But cabbage is high in antioxidants which are good for the heart and for fighting cancer. And raw cabbage is best as none of the nutrients are lost in cooking.

1 small head of green cabbage
2 carrots
1 small red or green pepper
1/2 cup silken tofu
1-2 tablespoons vinegar or lemon juice
1 tablespoon Dijon mustard
1 tablespoon chopped parsley
1/2 avocado (optional)
sea salt and pepper

Cut the cabbage in half, then make 1/4-inch slices of each half. Shred the carrots using either the shredding attachment of a food processor or a mandolin. Thinly slice the peppers, removing the seeds, spines, and stem. Put all the vegetables in a bowl. Blend the rest of the ingredients together until smooth and add to the vegetables. Toss until well covered and serve. The avocado adds flavor to the sauce, but as avocados are fatty, I wouldn't use it if I had other fat in the meal. You could also use a drop of olive oil.

Serves 4 to 6

Nutritional analysis per serving: 79 calories; 26.9 g fat (26.9% calories from fat); 0 mg cholesterol; 10.3 g carbohydrate; 6.3 g protein; 82 mg sodium; 196 mg calcium; 4.6 mg iron; 48 mg vitamin C

CUCUMBER SALAD WITH SOY DRESSING

This deceptively simple salad is not only delicious, but the dressing is low in calories and fat. Cucumbers sliced lengthwise in quarters can be served with the same dressing as a before dinner snack.

1 large or two medium cucumbers
1/2 teaspoon sesame oil
1 tablespoon soy sauce
1 tablespoon rice vinegar
1 tablespoon sesame seeds
1/2 teaspoon sucanat

Slice the cucumber very thin, with mandolin or food processor if possible. Mix all the other ingredients together and toss with the cucumbers.

Serves 4

> Nutritional analysis per serving: 61 calories; 2.1 g fat (27.3% calories from fat); 0 mg cholesterol; 9.7 g carbohydrate; 2.6 g protein; 263 mg sodium; 64 mg calcium; 1.2 mg iron; 15 mg vitamin C

SWEET AND SOUR CUCUMBER SALAD

Ordinarily this crisp and refreshing salad is made with more olive oil
and without the soy milk. This recipe helps cut down on fat.

3 cloves garlic, minced
3 tablespoons fresh dill, chopped (2 if dried)
1 teaspoon olive oil
1 tablespoon fat-free soy milk
2 tablespoons tarragon vinegar
1 tablespoon sucanat
1 large cucumber

Mix all the dressing ingredients in a bowl. Slice the cucumber very
thin in a processor or with a mandoline if possible. Add to the dressing and toss to cover.

Serves 2

Nutritional analysis per serving: 105 calories; 7.0 g fat (58.7% calories from
fat); 0 mg cholesterol; 9.8 g carbohydrate; 1.3 g protein; 26 mg sodium; 94 mg
calcium; 2.5 mg iron; 2 mg vitamin C

FISH-FREE SALAD NIÇOISE

This traditional Mediterranean salad from the south of France is typically made with tuna, but this is a fish-free version. Use chickpeas in place of tuna, if you wish. They are a wonderful source of protein, iron, and calcium.

3 potatoes
1 tablespoon olive oil
1 tablespoon soy milk or soy yogurt
2 tablespoons balsamic vinegar
1 tablespoon Dijon mustard
1 small red onion, chopped
3 cloves garlic, minced
1/4 cup chopped basil
2 tablespoons chopped parsley
1 head red leaf, green leaf, or Boston lettuce
1/3 lb. green beans
1 cucumber, sliced
1 tomato, sliced
1/2 cup cooked chickpeas (optional)

Boil the potatoes whole in their skins until cooked. Cut them in half lengthwise, then into 1/4-inch slices. Put the oil, vinegar, and mustard in a bowl and mix. Add the onion, garlic, and herbs. Add washed and dried lettuce, then the other vegetables, and toss.

Serves 4

Nutritional analysis per serving: 362 calories; 13.8 g fat (24.8% calories from fat); 0 mg cholesterol; 71.5 g carbohydrate; 22.5 g protein; 114 mg sodium; 301mg calcium; 8.9 mg iron; 77 mg vitamin C

GADO GADO

Gado Gado is an exotic Indonesian salad, partly cooked and partly raw, that is a meal in itself—perfect for a summer lunch. Or use it as an appetizer before a larger meal. The cauliflower, carrots, and cabbage are excellent sources of carotenes and other health-giving phytochemicals, so it is especially good for you.

1/2 head cauliflower
2 carrots, sliced
2 potatoes
1 cup shredded cabbage
1/4 lb. stringbeans or long beans
1/2 lb. tofu, in 1-inch cubes
1/4 lb. bean sprouts
1 small cucumber (kirby, if possible)
small head lettuce (Boston, red leaf, etc.)

Break the cauliflower into florets and slice the carrots and potatoes. Steam the potatoes for about 10 minutes. Add the carrots, cauliflower, cabbage, and stringbeans and steam for another 2 minutes. Then add the tofu and steam for another minute. Remove all from the heat and rinse in cold water. Put lettuce in the bottom of a bowl and top with other ingredients. Add the sauce.

Nutritional analysis per serving: 416 calories; 20.9 g fat (41.6% calories from fat); 0 mg cholesterol; 47.9 g carbohydrate; 18.1 g protein; 59 mg sodium; 194 mg calcium; 7.1 mg iron; 80 mg vitamin C

GADO GADO SAUCE

1/2 cup roasted peanuts, ground, or 1/4 cup peanut butter
1 teaspoon canola oil
2 shallots, minced
2 tablespoons water
2 cloves garlic, minced
1/4 teaspoon sucanat
2 tablespoons lemon or lime juice
1/2 cup coconut milk (optional) or water
1/4 teaspoon chili powder

Sauté the onions and garlic in small pan until soft, then add the peanuts (or peanut butter), sucanat, and chili powder. Add water and stir until smooth. Then add the coconut or extra water and blend. Remove from the heat and add the lemon or lime juice. Pour the sauce on the salad. Gado Gado is traditionally served with fried onions and shrimp chips on top. You might want to use some sliced scallions instead, or you can slice an onion into rounds and grill until brown.

Serves 4

GRILLED MUSHROOMS WITH ARUGULA

Portabello mushrooms are so thick and meaty that they can almost be thought of as a meat substitute. If no arugula is available, a mesclun mix of young lettuces will substitute. The mushrooms are also wonderful with white bean salad.

    5 cloves garlic
    3 sprigs fresh oregano (or 1 tablespoon dried)
    2 tablespoons rich vegetable broth
    1 teaspoon olive oil
    4 portabello mushrooms
    2 tablespoons balsamic vinegar
    1 bunch arugula

Mince the garlic and oregano and add to vegetable broth. Brush onto the gill side of the mushrooms. Place them, gill side up, on a grill or under a broiler and cook for about 5 minutes. The mushrooms should sweat their juices when they are ready. Slice into 1/4-inch slices. Place the arugula on a plate and cover with the mushrooms. Mix 1 tablespoon olive oil with balsamic vinegar and pour over the salad.

Serves 4

Nutritional analysis per serving: 42 calories; 1.8 g fat (33.5% calories from fat); 0 mg cholesterol; 6.3 g carbohydrate; 1.6 g protein; 55 mg sodium; 67 mg calcium; 2.1 mg iron; 3 mg vitamin C

JERUSALEM ARTICHOKE AND
SPINACH SALAD

Jerusalem artichoke, also known as sunchoke, is not an artichoke at all, but a root vegetable. The misnomer originates from the common perception that a Jerusalem artichoke tastes somewhat like an artichoke heart. A Jerusalem artichoke is usually served cooked, but in this case, it is thinly sliced and raw. Raw Jerusalem artichoke is sweet and crisp and makes an excellent foil for the leafy spinach. Spinach is one of the great sources of carotenes, vitamin C, and folic acid and is among the best foods you can eat. The soy parmesan should be casein-free.

3-4 Jerusalem artichokes
1 bunch spinach
2 cloves garlic, minced
2 tablespoons casein-free soy parmesan
1 tablespoon olive oil
1 tablespoon balsamic vinegar

Wash the Jerusalem artichokes well and slice very thinly, using a food processor or mandolin if possible. Thoroughly wash and dry the spinach. Put all the ingredients in a salad bowl and toss.
   Serves 4

Nutritional analysis per serving: 121 calories; 4.0 g fat (28.1% calories from fat); 0 mg cholesterol; 17.8 g carbohydrate; 5.5 g protein; 132 mg sodium; 454 mg calcium; 4.9 mg iron; 26 mg vitamin C

LENTIL SALAD

Here is another combination of the raw and the cooked. Most bean salads require advance planning as beans have to be soaked for so long. Lentils require no soaking, so you can be more spontaneous when you use them. This can be a meal unto itself.

1 cup lentils	1 tablespoon olive oil
2 cups water	2 tablespoons vinegar
bay leaf	2 tablespoons Dijon mustard
sprig of thyme	3 tablespoons chopped parsley
1 medium onion, chopped	1 tablespoon chopped oregano
4 cloves garlic, minced	1 ripe tomato, chopped
1 large carrot	lettuce leaves

Cook the lentils in fresh water to cover, with a bay leaf and a sprig of thyme for about half an hour or until soft. Drain and cool. Sauté the onion lightly in 1 tablespoon of oil, just to take off bitter edge, 30 seconds to 1 minute. Add the garlic for a few seconds more. Blanch the carrots in boiling water for a minute and drain. In a bowl, mix the oil, vinegar, and mustard until smooth. Add the sautéed onions and garlic, parsley, and oregano and mix until blended. Then add the lentils, tomatoes, and carrots, toss, and cool for about half an hour. Serve on a bed of lettuce.

Serves 4

Nutritional analysis per serving: 234 calories; 4.5 g fat (16.6% calories from fat); 0 mg cholesterol; 36.2 g carbohydrate; 15.1 g protein; 110 mg sodium; 96 mg calcium; 7.0 mg iron; 14 mg vitamin C

✿✿

MIXED SALAD WITH TAHINI DRESSING

Tahini is a paste made from sesame seeds and is very rich in nutrients, including calcium. This salad is resplendent with all the nutrients and antioxidants one needs to stay healthy.

> 2 tablespoons tahini
> 2 tablespoons water
> juice of lemon
> 1-2 tablespoons chopped dill
> 1/2 carrot, grated
> 3 cloves garlic, minced
> 1 head lettuce (red or green leaf, oak leaf, or Boston)
> 1 large cucumber, sliced
> 1 tomato, sliced
> 1/4 lb. tofu, cubed
> 1/4 lb. broccoli florets, steamed
> 1 carrot, shredded
> 1/2 cup sprouts

Put the tahini in a bowl and add the lemon juice. Stir together until thickened and add water slowly, until it has lost its pastiness. It shouldn't be too thin. Then add the dill, garlic, and grated carrot and stir until smooth. Add all the salad ingredients, toss, and serve.

> Serves 4

Nutritional analysis per serving: 161 calories; 7.5 g fat (37.4% calories from fat); 0 mg cholesterol; 18.1 g carbohydrate; 10.2 g protein; 40 mg sodium; 270 mg calcium; 7.4 mg iron; 60 mg vitamin C

MIZUNA AND HIJIKI SALAD
WITH SOY DRESSING

Hijiki is the sea vegetable richest in calcium, far surpassing milk as a source. Wakame and arame are close and similar in taste and texture to hijiki, but thicker. They would be good substitutes. Arame is second in delicacy and third in calcium content.

Mizuna is a ruffly leafed lettuce, somewhat bitter in taste, that recently has become very popular as part of a mesclun mix. For my taste it is a bit too bitter to stand alone, but works well in a mix and with the hijiki.

1 bunch mizuna
1-2 oz. hijiki, soaked in water
1 carrot, grated
1/2 teaspoon sesame oil
1 tablespoon soy sauce
1 tablespoon rice vinegar
1 tablespoon sesame seeds
1/2 teaspoon sucanat

The hijiki can be used as is after it has been soaked, but it is more delicate if it is braised. Place it and its soaking liquid in a pan and cook over low heat for just a minute or two, then chill. Divide the mizuna onto four plates, layering the grated carrot and the hijiki on top of it. Mix the other ingredients together and pour over the salad.

Serves 4

Nutritional analysis per serving: 123 calories; 4.0 g fat (29.3% calories from fat); 0 mg cholesterol; 16.5 g carbohydrate; 5.3 g protein; 561 mg sodium; 442 mg calcium; 6.9 mg iron; 21 mg vitamin C

❀❀

POTATO SALAD

Like coleslaw, potato salad is a standard that is usually heavily laden with mayonnaise, which contains eggs (usually raw eggs). This version gives a substitute for the mayonnaise, but is not a substitute for taste.

VEGETABLES
4 potatoes
1 carrot
1 leek
1 kirby cucumber
2 tablespoons chopped dill

SOY MAYONNAISE
1/4 lb. silken tofu
1 tablespoon olive oil
2 tablespoons Dijon mustard
2 tablespoons tarragon vinegar

Wash the potatoes well. There are so many nutrients in the skin that I almost never peel them. Boil until tender and slice lengthwise. Then cut into 1/4-inch slices and put in a salad bowl. Blanch the carrot just for a minute. Slice the carrot, leek, and cucumber and add to the potatoes. Mix the dill and the ingredients for soy mayonnaise, then mix with the vegetables.

Serves 2 to 4

Nutritional analysis per serving: 269 calories; 1.7 g fat (5.3% calories from fat); 0 mg cholesterol; 57.9 g carbohydrate; 8.9 g protein; 126 mg sodium; 102 mg calcium; 4.6 mg iron; 64 mg vitamin C

ROASTED POTATO SALAD WITH
SUN-DRIED TOMATOES

Roasting the potatoes gives them a richer, meatier taste than boiling. Don't peel the potatoes, but scrub them clean. Many nutrients, such as potassium, are found in the skin.

4 potatoes
1 red onion or 4-5 shallots, unpeeled
sprig or 2 of thyme
1 tablespoon olive oil
4 cloves garlic, unpeeled
1/4 cup sun-dried tomatoes, soaked in water
2 tablespoons balsamic vinegar
1 tablespoon Dijon mustard
2 tablespoons fat-free soy milk or soy yogurt
about 10 black olives (optional)
2 sprigs basil or oregano, chopped (2 tablespoons if dried)

Quarter the potatoes and onion. If using shallots, leave them whole with skin on. Put the potatoes in a baking pan with the onion or shallots. Sprinkle with thyme and drizzle with 1 tablespoon olive oil. Add sea salt. Bake in a 350° oven for about 15 minutes. Add the garlic and bake until all ingredients are soft (about 15 minutes). Remove from the heat and cool.

Cut the sun-dried tomatoes into quarters. Skin the shallots and garlic and cut the shallots in half, or the onion in slices. Cut the potatoes into 1/2-inch slices. Slice the olives. Mix. Add the soy milk, vinegar, mustard vinegar, and herbs and toss. Add salt and pepper to taste. Serve on a bed of lettuce. *Serves 4*

Nutritional analysis per serving: 357 calories; 8.2 g fat (17.8% calories from fat); 0 mg cholesterol; 68.8 g carbohydrate; 16.7 g protein; 2409 mg sodium; 232 mg calcium; 14.0 mg iron; 47 mg vitamin C

SWEET POTATO SALAD WITH
ORANGE DRESSING

This recipe is extremely rich in beta-carotene and vitamins A and C. In fact, sweet potatoes have a whopping amount of vitamin A, higher than any other food. Yams do not. A yam is an African root vegetable that looks just like a sweet potato. This often results in confusion between the two. The Indian version of this dish would be made with a lot of oil, which I find unnecessary and have eliminated.

4 sweet potatoes or yams
juice of 1/2 orange
juice of 1/2 lime or lemon
3 tablespoons maple syrup
1-inch piece ginger, minced
5 tablespoons minced coriander
2 cloves garlic, minced (optional)
lettuce or mesclun mix

Slice the sweet potatoes and steam. Cool and julienne. Mix the other ingredients except the lettuce to make a dressing. Place the sweet potatoes in a bowl and cover with the dressing. Serve on a bed of lettuce or mesclun.
Serves 4

Nutritional analysis per serving: 158 calories; 0.5 g fat (2.8% calories from fat); 0 mg cholesterol; 37.4 g carbohydrate; 2.4 g protein; 20 mg sodium; 72 mg calcium; 1.8 mg iron; 48 mg vitamin C

THAI-VIETNAMESE SALAD

Most of these salad recipes have been adapted to eliminate the oil. One wonderful thing about this one is that it was never intended to have oil. This is the traditional Thai-Vietnamese way of making a salad dressing, and it is crisp and delicious.

1 head lettuce (red or green leaf, oak leaf, etc.)
1 cucumber
1 carrot
1 cup Asian bean sprouts
1-2 sprigs mint
1-2 sprigs coriander
2 tablespoons soy sauce or fish sauce
2 tablespoons water
1 tablespoon lime juice
1/2 teaspoon sucanat
2 cloves garlic, minced
pinch of chili powder

Wash and dry the lettuce, separate it into leaves, and put it into a bowl. Slice the cucumber thinly and add it to the bowl. Shred the carrot into very fine julienne strips (in a processor or mandolin) and add, with bean sprouts and herbs, to the bowl. Mix all other ingredients together, pour over the salad and toss.

Serves 2

Nutritional analysis per serving: 107 calories; 2.9 g fat (21.7% calories from fat); 2 mg cholesterol; 18.7 g carbohydrate; 4.6 g protein; 24 mg sodium; 84 mg calcium; 2.3 mg iron; 44 mg vitamin C

WHEAT BERRY SALAD

We tend to ignore many wonderful, healthful grains. Here's a great idea for one of them. The fruits, nuts, and vegetables mixed together with the wheat berries lend a sweet and sour flavor and a crunchy texture to the dish. You could also use quinoa or couscous.

1 cup wheat berries
3 scallions, sliced
1/4 cup raisins or currants
1/4 cup dried apricots, chopped
1 small cucumber, chopped
1/4 cup chopped walnuts or almonds
2 tablespoons chopped parsley
2 tablespoons chopped dill
2 tablespoons olive oil
2 tablespoons lemon juice or vinegar
lettuce

Cook the wheat berries in 2 cups water for about 1 hour. Cool and put in a bowl with the other ingredients. Toss and serve on a bed of lettuce.

Variation: Use quinoa instead of wheat berries. Quinoa is a Peruvian grain that is much finer than the wheat berries and very high in protein. It requires less cooking time, about 15 minutes. When cooking quinoa, be careful not to let it get mushy.

Serves 2 to 4

Nutritional analysis per serving: 316 calories; 26.2 g fat (69.2% calories from fat); 0 mg cholesterol; 19.4 g carbohydrate; 6.8 g protein; 169 mg sodium; 77 mg calcium; 2.8 mg iron; 16 mg vitamin C

❈ ❈

WHITE BEAN SALAD

Bean salads are a wonderful and delicious way of getting protein. White beans are exceptionally rich in potassium and iron.

1 cup cannelli beans or other white beans
2 cups water
bay leaf
sprig of thyme and sage
1 medium red onion, chopped
1 tablespoon olive oil
8-10 sun-dried tomatoes soaked in water, or
  a roasted red pepper
3 garlic cloves, minced
1/4 cup chopped basil
2 tablespoons vinegar
sea salt and pepper to taste

Soak the beans in water overnight or for the day. Cook them in fresh water with the herbs (except basil) until soft, for about an hour. Sauté the onion lightly in 1 tablespoon of oil, just to take off the bitter edge, about 30 seconds to 1 minute. Add the garlic for a few seconds more. Drain the sun-dried tomatoes, reserving the water, and chop coarsely. Mix oil and vinegar and a little of the reserved sun-dried tomato water in a bowl with garlic and onions. Add beans and mix thoroughly. Add the sun-dried tomatoes, basil, and salt and pepper if desired. Toss and serve on a bed of lettuce.

Serves 4

Nutritional analysis per serving: 508 calories; 7.3 g fat (11.6% calories from fat); 0 mg cholesterol; 97.7 g carbohydrate; 28.2 g protein; 2274 mg sodium; 304 mg calcium; 17.3 mg iron; 48 mg vitamin C

SALAD DRESSINGS

If you are on a low-fat, dairy-free diet, salads may seem like a wonderful escape from all of the diet restrictions. This is often true if you don't take the dressings into account. When you realize that, on the average, oils contain 120 calories per table-spoon, you see that salads aren't even good for weight loss diets. For this reason I offer a variety of salad dressings, classic and new, that are low in fat, dairy-free, healthful, and delicious.

MUSTARD VINAIGRETTE

This is a fairly standard dressing, lighter on the olive oil than usual. Should the dressing not go far enough, add a few tablespoons of soy milk.

1 tablespoon olive oil
2 tablespoons soy milk
2 tablespoons tarragon wine vinegar
1 tablespoon Dijon mustard
1 tablespoon chopped parsley
1 tablespoon chopped tarragon, basil, or both
1 tablespoon capers (optional)
1 chopped shallot
pinch sea salt

Mix all the ingredients together in a bowl.

Oil Alternative: Use 2 tablespoons silken tofu in place of olive oil.
    Serves 2

Nutritional analysis per serving: 82 calories; 7.4 g fat (77.2 calories from fat); 0 mg cholesterol; 3.6 g carbohydrate; 1.3 g protein; 140 mg sodium; 30 mg calcium; 0.9 mg iron; 7 mg vitamin C

ROASTED RED PEPPER VINAIGRETTE

As there is rarely enough dressing for a large salad if the olive oil is kept to a minimum, this roasted pepper purée adds liquid and, at the same time, makes an extra delicious dressing.

1 tablespoon olive oil (optional)
2 tablespoons vinegar
1 roasted red pepper, with its juice, seeds, and stem removed
2 cloves garlic
pinch sea salt
5-10 basil leaves

Purée all ingredients in a food processor.
Serves 2

Nutritional analysis per serving: 77 calories; 6.9 g fat (75.3% calories from fat); 0 mg cholesterol; 4.4 g carbohydrate; 0.7 g protein; 2 mg sodium; 19 mg calcium; 0.5 mg iron; 72 mg vitamin C

TOFU DRESSING

This dressing eliminates oil entirely and is rich in protein. Many people feel that tofu is great for fighting cancer and reducing cholesterol. This is a way for people who don't like tofu to eat it without even knowing it.

1/4 lb. tofu (silken is best)
1/2 cup fat-free soy milk
2 teaspoons herb vinegar (raspberry, tarragon, champagne, etc.)
1 tablespoon Dijon mustard

Mash the tofu or purée it in a food processor. Add the other ingredients and mix well. A variety of herbs can be added: parsley, tarragon, basil, dill. Add 1 chopped sprig each to the dressing.
Serves 2 to 4

Nutritional analysis per serving: 46 calories; 2.0 g fat (37.2% calories from fat); 0 mg cholesterol; 3.9 g carbohydrate; 3.8 g protein; 65 mg sodium; 61mg calcium; 2.2 mg iron; 2 mg vitamin C

CITRUS DRESSING

This is delicious with julienned sweet potatoes. It is also excellent with other vegetables and fruits, such as avocado and grapefruit. The citrus juices are not only a great replacement for the oil, but an excellent source of vitamins, too, and extremely delicious.

3 tablespoons orange juice
3 tablespoons lime juice
1-inch piece of ginger, minced
2 tablespoons maple syrup
1 tablespoon olive oil
1 tablespoon chopped parsley or coriander
2 cloves minced garlic (optional)

Put all the ingredients in a bowl and whisk together.
Serves 2 to 4

Nutritional analysis per serving: 48 calories; 0.1 g fat (1.7% calories from fat); 0 mg cholesterol; 12.3 g carbohydrate; 0.3 g protein; 3 mg sodium; 21 mg calcium; 0.3 mg iron; 13 mg vitamin C

TAHINI DRESSING

Tahini is made of ground sesame seeds. It is rich in calcium and less fatty than oils. However, it is still high in fat and calories and should be used in small quantities.

2 tablespoons tahini
2 tablespoons water
juice of lemon
1-2 tablespoons chopped dill
1/2 carrot, grated
2 cloves garlic, minced

Put the tahini in a bowl and add the lemon juice and water. Stir until smooth. Then add the other ingredients and mix together. If too thick, add a little more water slowly, whisking until it reaches the desired consistency.

Serves 2

Nutritional analysis per serving: 114 calories; 8.2 g fat (59.8% calories from fat); 0 mg cholesterol; 9.0 g carbohydrate; 3.5 g protein; 10 mg sodium; 178 mg calcium; 3.6 mg iron; 13 mg vitamin C

SOY DRESSING

This dressing can be used with a variety of salads and as a dip. It is most commonly used with thinly sliced cucumbers.

1/2 teaspoon sesame oil
1 tablespoon soy sauce
1 tablespoon rice vinegar
1 tablespoon sesame seeds
1/2 teaspoon sucanat

Mix all the ingredients together.
    Serves 2

Nutritional analysis per serving: 45 calories; 3.3 g fat (64.1% calories from fat); 0 mg cholesterol; 3.0 g carbohydrate; 1.2 g protein; 517 mg sodium; 46 mg calcium; 0.9 mg iron; 0 mg vitamin C

SAUCES AND SPREADS

AIOLI

Aioli is basically a garlic mayonnaise without the mustard. Again, the traditional dish is made with eggs, while here silken tofu is the replacement. I enliven the recipe with sun-dried tomatoes.

1/4 lb. silken tofu
juice of 1 lemon
3 cloves garlic
6 sun-dried tomatoes, soaked in water
salt and pepper
1 tablespoon olive oil

Place all of the ingredients in a food processor or blender and blend until smooth.
Serves 2 to 4

Nutritional analysis per serving: 355 calories; 9.5 g fat (20.8% calories from fat); 0 mg cholesterol; 63.1 g carbohydrate; 18.5 g protein; 2266 mg sodium; 164 mg calcium; 11.9 mg iron; 50 mg vitamin C

ROUILLE

This is another garlic mayonnaise, usually served with bouillabaisse. However, it has many other uses, such as a dip for crudités. This time, bread replaces the egg as a thickener—a more traditional method of preparation.

4 cloves garlic
1 tablespoon olive oil
1 large slice whole wheat bread
juice of a lemon
1/2 teaspoon cayenne
pinch of saffron
pinch of salt

Soak the bread in water until soft. Remove the crust and squeeze out the water. Place all ingredients in a blender or food processor and blend until smooth.

Serves 2

Nutritional analysis per serving: 126 calories; 7.7 g fat (51.9% calories from fat); 0 mg cholesterol; 13.5 g carbohydrate; 2.5 g protein; 112 mg sodium; 27 mg calcium; 0.8 mg iron; 12 mg vitamin C

SOY MAYONNAISE

The major problem with mayonnaise is that it is made with raw egg yolks, which are heavy with cholesterol and may be a source of salmonella. Silken tofu is an excellent substitute, giving the sauce the needed thickness without the problems while adding protein.

1/4 lb. tofu (silken tofu is a good choice)
1 tablespoon olive oil
2 tablespoons Dijon mustard
2 tablespoons tarragon vinegar

Blend all ingredients in a food processor or mash the tofu in a bowl and whisk in the other ingredients.

Variations: Add 2 to 3 tablespoons of finely chopped herbs, choosing from among the following: parsley, tarragon, basil, oregano, dill; 3 cloves garlic, minced; or 2 chopped shallots.

Serves 2

Nutritional analysis per serving: 129 calories; 10.3 g fat (66.8% calories from fat); 0 mg cholesterol; 5.4 g carbohydrate; 6.1 g protein; 194 mg sodium; 108 mg calcium; 4.3 mg iron; 1 mg vitamin C

GARLIC LEMON SAUCE

3 cloves garlic
juice of a lemon
sea salt
1 tablespoon olive oil
1/4 cup silken tofu

Mince the garlic and blend with the other ingredients.
    Serves 2

Nutritional analysis per serving: 95 calories; 8.2 g fat (73.5% calories from fat); 0 mg cholesterol; 3.8 g carbohydrate; 2.8 g protein; 3 mg sodium; 41 mg calcium; 1.8 mg iron; 12 mg vitamin C

OLIVATA

This Mediterranean sauce is often used in the preparation of fish, but it is also great as a sauce for crudités, bread, or artichokes.

4 cloves garlic, chopped
1 teaspoon olive oil (optional)
1/4 lb. pitted calamata olives
1/4 cup sun-dried tomatoes soaked in 1 cup water
2 tablespoons chopped basil

Sauté the garlic in olive oil for about 2 minutes. Purée all the ingredients in a food processor. Serve with bread, crackers, or crudités. If you leave out the oil, add a little of the tomato water.
    Serves 4 to 6

Nutritional analysis per serving: 317 calories; 6.6 g fat (15.9% calories from fat); 0 mg cholesterol; 62.5 g carbohydrate; 15.7 g protein; 2461 mg sodium147 mg calcium; 10.7 mg iron; 44 mg vitamin C

GUACAMOLE

This Mexican dip for taco chips needs no alterations for a vegan diet. Although avocados are high in fat, they are rich in nutrients, and occasional use is fine. Everyone has a favorite way of preparing guacamole, and this is mine.

> *2 ripe avocados*
> *1 small red onion, chopped, or 4 scallions, chopped*
> *juice of 1/2 lemon*
> *1/4 teaspoon cayenne pepper or 1 jalapeño pepper, chopped*
> *2 tablespoons chopped cilantro*
> *1 tomato, chopped*

Peel the avocados, cut them in half, and remove the pit. Place in a bowl and mash well. Add the other ingredients and continue mashing until all the ingredients are well mixed, but still a bit chunky.

> *Serves 2 to 4*

Nutritional analysis per serving: 181 calories; 15.3 g fat (69.6% calories from fat); 0 mg cholesterol; 12.4 g carbohydrate; 2.6 g protein; 12 mg sodium; 22 mg calcium; 1.1 mg iron; 16 mg vitamin C

SPINACH DIP WITH SOY YOGURT

Served with pita bread or crudités, this fragrant Persian dip is heavenly. And spinach, as already pointed out, is a great source of the antioxidant beta-carotene. Soy yogurt is a source of protein and calcium.

1 lb. spinach, carefully washed
5 shallots, chopped
1 teaspoon olive oil
1 cup soy yogurt
1/4 teaspoon ground nutmeg
1 tablespoon chopped dill
pinch sea salt

Steam the spinach for just a few minutes until it wilts. Drain, squeeze out the water, and chop finely (can be done in food processor). Chop the shallots and sauté in olive oil (or use minced roasted shallots). Add the spinach and cook for a minute or two. Put the yogurt in a bowl and add the spinach mix, nutmeg, dill, and salt and stir together until smooth.

Serves 6 to 8

Nutritional analysis per serving: 43 calories; 1.1 g fat (20.5% calories from fat); 0 mg cholesterol; 6.3 g carbohydrate; 3.1 g protein; 44 mg sodium; 59 mg calcium; 1.5 mg iron; 13 mg vitamin C

HUMMUS WITH TAHINI

This Middle Eastern dip is usually a part of a medley of appetizers in a Middle Eastern meal. Often tabouli, yogurt, and babaganoush complement it. However, hummus stands extremely well on its own. The chickpeas and parsley are a great source of protein, iron, and calcium. The tahini is also rich in calcium.

1 cup chickpeas
1 cup tahini
juice of 1 lemon
2 cloves garlic
3-4 sprigs parsley
1/2 teaspoon cumin
sea salt to taste
2 tablespoons pine nuts

Soak the chickpeas overnight. When ready to cook, place the drained chickpeas in a pot, covering them with fresh water. Bring to boil and lower the heat to simmer. Cook until soft, about one hour. (You may use canned chickpeas instead, but I find them harder to digest.) Chop enough parsley to make about a tablespoon. Place all ingredients except the pine nuts in a processor and blend until smooth. Lightly sauté the pine nuts in a drop of sesame oil (or in a non-stick pan without oil) until lightly browned. Place the hummus in a bowl and sprinkle parsley and pine nuts on top.

Serves 4 to 6

Nutritional analysis per serving: 401 calories; 25.2 g fat (53.2% calories from fat); 0 mg cholesterol; 34.4 g carbohydrate; 15.5 g protein; 25 mg sodium; 477mg calcium; 11.9 mg iron; 35 mg vitamin C

EGGPLANT DIP (GREEK MELITZANASALATA)

This dish can be served with pita bread or used as a dip for crudités. It is often made like a mayonnaise, heavy with olive oil and eggs. This is a lighter version. The method of cooking the eggplant makes it soft and perfect as a sauce.

1 large eggplant
1 small onion
2-3 stems parsley
juice of 1/2 lemon
1 tablespoon olive oil (optional)
salt and pepper to taste

Char the whole eggplant on top of a stove burner, turning it continuously as each side gets charred (see "Spicy Eggplant" on page 185 in "Vegetables as Side Dishes"). Keep an eye on it as it cooks much faster than you would expect. The charred skin adds a smoky taste to the eggplant. When cooked on all sides and soft inside, remove it from the stove and let it cool. Remove the skin. You may leave just a little on for flavor, but charred foods can be carcinogenic. Put the soft pulpy part in a food processor and add the other ingredients. Blend until creamy. I recently made this with lime juice rather than lemon and it was wonderful, if not traditional.

Variation (called Babaganoush): Follow the recipe above but use 2 tablespoons tahini in place of olive oil; 3 cloves garlic; and 2-3 tablespoons pine nuts.

Serves 4 to 6

Nutritional analysis per serving: 156 calories; 4.5 g fat (22.0% calories from fat); 0 mg cholesterol; 26.4 g carbohydrate; 9.2 g protein; 166 mg sodium; 540 mg calcium; 35.5 mg iron; 51 mg vitamin C

PEANUT SAUCE

This sauce is used with Vietnamese Spring Rolls. However, if thinned, it can be used as a salad dressing or as a dip. Peanuts may contain aflatoxins, so consume them in moderation.

1/4 cup ground peanuts
1/2 cup hoisin sauce
1 small chili pepper, seeded and sliced
2 cloves garlic, minced
1 teaspoon oil (soy, safflower, sesame, or canola)
1/2 cup water
2 tablespoons fish sauce (optional)

Sauté the garlic in the oil and add the other ingredients. Stir until smooth. Use soy sauce if you don't wish to use the fish sauce. Add extra water for a thinner sauce.

Serves 4 to 6

Nutritional analysis per serving: 121 calories; 8.9 g fat (64.0% calories from fat); 4 mg cholesterol; 9.2 g carbohydrate; 2.2 g protein; 3 mg sodium; 10 mg calcium; 0.5 mg iron; 23 mg vitamin C

YELLOW SPLIT PEA PURÉE

This is a wonderful alternative to butter. You can put it on the table as a spread, use it on sandwiches, or use it as a dip.

1 cup dried yellow split peas
2 cups water
1/2 onion, chopped
6 cloves garlic
1 bay leaf
2 sprigs rosemary (optional)
juice of 1 lemon
1 tablespoon olive oil (optional)

Soak the peas for a day and cook in water with all the other dry ingredients until soft, about 15 minutes. Purée in a food processor with the lemon juice and (optional) olive oil. The rosemary adds extra flavor, but the recipe works well without it. The olive oil adds liquid and a rich flavor, but it, too, can be left out if you want to avoid fat. You can use a tablespoon or two of a rich vegetable broth in its place.

Serves 6 to 8

Nutritional analysis per serving: 96 calories; 0.5 g fat (4.0% calories from fat); 0 mg cholesterol; 17.8 g carbohydrate; 6.4 g protein; 5 mg sodium; 32 mg calcium; 1.5 mg iron; 7 mg vitamin C

MUSTARD SAUCE

This wonderful sauce is great on a veggie burger, baked tofu, tempeh, or seitan. You can also cook the tempeh, baked tofu, or seitan right in the sauce.

>*2 cloves minced garlic*
>*1 tablespoon chopped onion or shallot*
>*1 teaspoon olive oil*
>*1 tablespoon whole wheat flour*
>*1 teaspoon arrowroot*
>*1/2 cup fat-free soy milk*
>*2 tablespoons Dijon mustard*
>*juice of 1/2 lemon (about 2 tablespoons)*
>*1 tablespoon dry sherry (optional)*
>*1 tablespoon chopped tarragon*
>*1 tablespoon chopped parsley*

Sauté the onion and garlic in olive oil on very low heat until transparent. Put the flour and arrowroot in a small bowl and slowly add the soy milk, whisking with a wire whisk or fork to prevent lumps. Add to the pan and keep stirring until smooth and thickened. Add the mustard (optional), sherry, and lemon juice and keep stirring. If too thick, add a little more soy milk. Stir in the herbs and serve.

Nutritional analysis per serving: 95 calories; 3.2 g fat (28.5% calories from fat); 0 mg cholesterol; 15.1 g carbohydrate; 2.9 g protein; 191 mg sodium; 77 mg calcium; 1.5 mg iron; 13 mg vitamin C

SOUPS

A well-seasoned vegetable stock makes a meat or poultry-based stock totally unnecessary. And there is no fat. Making a vegetable stock can be a way to use parts of vegetables that you might otherwise throw away, like the stems of broccoli or asparagus. Some people keep a stockpot, and if you are inclined to do so, just keep throwing in those vegetable parts and keep it going all the time.

VEGETABLE STOCK

1 large onion, chopped
6 cloves garlic
1 large carrot, sliced
1-2 celery stalks, sliced
1 leek, sliced
1 turnip, cubed
2 bay leaves
sprig of thyme, or 1/2 teaspoon dried thyme
large sprig parsley
few sage leaves
mushroom stems (if available)
any leftover vegetable parts, such as peeled broccoli,
 cauliflower stalks, or tomatoes
5 quarts water
sea salt
a few white peppercorns (optional)

Boil water in a stockpot and add all the ingredients. Simmer for at least half an hour. For a richer stock, roast the onions and garlic in the oven for about half an hour before putting them into the stockpot.

Variation: For a richer stock, sprinkle the onions, a head of garlic, and a leek with thyme and roast in a pan at 450° until soft, about half an hour. Then add to the stockpot.

✿✿

MUSHROOM WATER STOCK

2 cups mushroom soaking water (left from soaking shitakes),
   plus
shitake mushroom stems and any other mushroom stems and
   pieces you may have, plus
2 slices ginger
1 small onion, sliced
1 garlic clove
2 scallions, sliced
1 sprig parsley
1 small carrot, sliced
1 stalk celery, sliced

Put the mushroom water in a pot and bring to a boil. Reduce the
heat and add the other ingredients. Simmer for 20 to 30 minutes.

PUMPKIN SOUP

Pumpkin is a member of the squash family. This and its orange coloring indicate a high level of beta-carotene. While not as rich in vitamin A as some other vegetables, it is still a very legitimate source.

4 cups stock
2 cups pumpkin, peeled and chopped
1 onion, chopped
1 fennel stalk, chopped
1 tablespoon sage
pinch of cayenne
1 teaspoon nutmeg
1 cup fat-free soy milk
1 tablespoon minced parsley
2 tablespoons toasted pine nuts

Put the broth in a pot and bring to a boil. Reduce the heat and add the pumpkin, fennel, and onion. Add the seasonings and cook until the vegetables are soft. Add the soy milk and stir until the soup boils. Purée in a blender. Put in bowls and top with a sprinkle of parsley and pine nuts.

Serves 6

Nutritional analysis per serving: 160 calories; 4.2 g fat (22.8% calories from fat); 2 mg cholesterol; 26.0 g carbohydrate; 5.9 g protein; 1109 mg sodium; 64 mg calcium; 2.1 mg iron; 11 mg vitamin C

RED PEPPER SOUP

This soup is smooth and delicious. Red peppers are a good source of vitamin A. Leeks are only a modest source of vitamin A, while scallions are very high in it. Should you want to increase your vitamin A intake, substitute scallions for leeks.

> 5 roasted red peppers
> 4 shallots, chopped
> 1 small leek, chopped
> 2 cloves garlic, minced
> 1 teaspoon olive oil
> 6 cups broth
> 1 teaspoon thyme
> 3/4 cups fat-free soy milk
> salt and pepper to taste
> 5 tablespoons chopped basil

Peel, seed, and slice the peppers. Sauté the shallots, leek, and garlic in olive oil until transparent. Add the broth, thyme, and peppers and simmer 5 to 10 minutes. Purée and return to the pot. Add the soy milk, salt, and pepper and cook for a few minutes more. Place in bowls and sprinkle fresh basil on top.

Serves 6

Nutritional analysis per serving: 218 calories; 4.9 g fat (19.6% calories from fat); 2 mg cholesterol; 37.2g carbohydrate; 7.7 g protein; 1658 mg sodium; 78 mg calcium; 3.2 mg iron; 127 mg vitamin C

LENTIL SOUP

Lentils are easier to use than other beans as they don't require soaking. Like bean salads, bean soups are a good source of protein.

> *1 onion, chopped*
> *5 cloves garlic, chopped*
> *1 teaspoon olive oil*
> *1 cup lentils, uncooked*
> *1 bay leaf*
> *sprig of thyme*
> *sprig of parsley, chopped*
> *1 tablespoon cumin*
> *6 cups stock or water*
> *3 tomatoes, chopped*
> *1 small red pepper, chopped*

Sauté the onions and garlic in olive oil until soft. Add the lentils and stir until coated. Add the herbs and spices. Then add the stock, bring to a boil, and reduce heat to a simmer. Next, add the tomatoes and peppers and cook until the lentils are soft, about half an hour. The cumin gives the soup a Middle Eastern flavor. For a Mediterranean flavor use oregano and basil instead.

Variation: You may add soy bacon to the soup for a more traditional flavor.
> *Serves 6*

Nutritional analysis per serving: 343 calories; 5.1g fat (12.8% calories from fat); 2 mg cholesterol; 59.2 g carbohydrate; 18.7 g protein; 1711 mg sodium; 238 mg calcium; 17.7 mg iron; 58 mg vitamin C

PERSIAN MIXED BEAN SOUP

This is a recipe from my friend Monir Farmanfarmaian. She prefers to use butter and meat, as is the Persian custom, but she adapted the recipe to our needs. It is so fragrant and delicious that I don't know why anyone would want to ruin it with meat.

The beans, rice, and greens in this recipe make it one of the most healthful meals you can have, filled with iron, calcium, carotenes, protein, and antioxidants.

1/2 cup dried chickpeas
1/2 cup dried black-eyed peas or white beans
1/2 cup dried yellow split peas
1/2 cup small red kidney beans
1/2 cup lentils
1/4 cup brown basmati rice
2 medium onions, chopped
6 cloves garlic, chopped
1 tablespoon olive oil (optional)
1 bunch scallions or 1 large leek, chopped
1 bunch parsley
1 bunch dill
1 sprig basil
1 bunch coriander
1 lb. spinach, washed and chopped
2 tablespoons cinnamon
2 tablespoons cumin
2 tablespoons turmeric
2 tablespoons dried mint (fresh is ok)
salt and pepper to taste

continued

Soak the beans in water for 8 hours or more and the rice for at least an hour (the lentils and split peas don't have to be soaked). Sauté the onion and garlic in olive oil slowly until golden. Add 6 to 8 cups of water, the rice, and half the split peas. Cook for about an hour. The peas and rice serve as a thickener for the soup, and essentially should dissolve. Add the chickpeas, the lentils, the remaining split peas, and the beans and cook another 30 minutes. Add more water, if necessary.

Chop the herbs roughly, including some stems. Then add the scallions or leeks, chopped spinach, parsley, coriander, basil, dill, and the spices and cook until all of the beans are tender. Sprinkle on the mint and add more cinnamon, if necessary. Stir frequently during cooking.

Serves 6 to 8

Nutritional analysis per serving: 289 calories; 2.4 g fat (7.0% calories from fat); 0 mg cholesterol; 52.4 g carbohydrate; 18.9 g protein; 84 mg sodium; 298 mg calcium; 15.9 mg iron; 29 mg vitamin C

BLACK BEAN SOUP

The soy bacon (Canadian or American-style) in this recipe is a fat-free, meat-free substitute for the real thing, and surprisingly good.

1 red onion, chopped
6 cloves garlic, chopped
1 tablespoon olive oil
2 jalapeño peppers, chopped
1 carrot, sliced
4 cups stock
1 cup black beans, soaked for a day
4 tablespoons chopped parsley
1 sweet red pepper
1/2 cup sherry (optional)
4 oz. soy bacon
1/4 teaspoon allspice
4 tablespoons chopped coriander

Sauté the onions and garlic in a kettle in olive oil until golden. Add the jalapeño peppers and carrots and stir for a few minutes. Add the stock and bring to a boil. Add the beans and the parsley and simmer for about half an hour. Cut the red pepper into small pieces, removing the ribs and seeds. Add to the pot along with the soy bacon, allspice, and sherry. Cook until the beans are very soft. Remove 1 slotted spoonful of the beans and purée the rest. Put the soup into bowls and top each with some of the solid beans and a sprinkling of coriander.
   Serves 4 to 6

Nutritional analysis per serving: 320 calories; 5.5 g fat (13.9% calories from fat); 2 mg cholesterol; 58.7 g carbohydrate; 17.4 g protein; 1295 mg sodium; 85 mg calcium; 3.6mg iron; 60 mg vitamin C

POTATO-LEEK SOUP

This is one of the few French classics in the book, with soy milk substituting for cream.

2 leeks, chopped
1 teaspoon olive oil
4 potatoes, sliced
4 cups stock
4 tablespoons chopped parsley
4 tablespoons chopped tarragon
1 cup fat-free soy milk
1 teaspoon ground nutmeg

Sauté the leeks in the olive oil until soft. Add the potatoes, nutmeg, and stock and cook until potatoes are soft. Add the herbs and soy milk and simmer for a few more minutes. Remove the vegetables with a slotted spoon and put in a blender with about 1 cup of the liquid. Purée and return to the pot with the rest of the stock. Stir well, correct the seasonings, and serve.

Serves 4

Nutritional analysis per serving: 442 calories; 6.0 g fat (11.9% calories from fat); 2 mg cholesterol; 85.8 g carbohydrate; 14.0 g protein; 1679 mg sodium; 156 mg calcium; 6.5 mg iron; 68 mg vitamin C

MUSHROOM SOUP

This dish is wonderful without any substitutions. You don't need cream as the mushrooms are so good. Add some shitake mushrooms for your health.

4 cups mushroom stock
1 lb. white mushrooms, or a variety of mushrooms, sliced
1 large leek, chopped
1 small yellow onion, chopped
1 tablespoon olive oil
5 cloves garlic, chopped
1 small carrot, chopped
1 large potato, cut in cubes
2 tablespoons chopped tarragon
2 tablespoons chopped parsley
2 tablespoons chopped dill
salt and pepper

Strain the stock and warm it in a stockpot. Sauté the mushrooms in olive oil until soft. Remove from the pan and add the onion and leeks. Cook until transparent and add the garlic, cooking for another minute or two. Reserve a tablespoon or two of the mushrooms. Add the sautéed ingredients to the stock with the carrots and potato and cook until soft. Reserve some of the herbs for garnish and add the rest to the stock with the salt and pepper. Cook for another minute or two. Remove the vegetables with a slotted spoon and place in a blender or food processor with about 1/2 cup of the stock. Purée and return to the pot, stirring until smooth. Serve in bowls, garnishing with the reserved mushrooms and herbs. *Serves 4 to 6*

Nutritional analysis per serving: 308 calories; 8.1 g fat (22.8% calories from fat); 2 mg cholesterol; 50.8 g carbohydrate; 11.2 g protein; 1676 mg sodium; 121 mg calcium; 5.9 mg iron; 28 mg vitamin C

THAI COCONUT SOUP

Chicken soup is supposed to be the panacea for all ills. What can you do if you don't eat chicken? The ginger, lemongrass, and lime in this soup replace the chicken.

> 6-8 *shitake mushrooms soaked in water until soft*
> 6 *cups stock with the water from soaked shitake mushrooms*
> 1/4 *lb. snow peas*
> 1/4 *lb. tofu in 1/2-inch cubes*
> 1 *small carrot, sliced*
> 5 *tablespoons soy sauce or fish sauce*
> 1 *cup coconut milk*
> 2-inch *piece ginger or galangal thinly sliced*
>   206(*galangal is a root, similar to ginger*)*
> 3 *stalks lemongrass, thinly sliced**
> 1 *chili pepper, thinly sliced*
> 3 *lime leaves, sliced**
> *juice of 1 lemon*
> *coriander leaves for garnish*

Place the stock in a pot and bring to a boil. Reduce the heat and add carrots, shitake mushrooms, galangal or ginger, lemon grass, lime leaves, and soy or fish sauce. Cook on low heat until carrots are tender. Add coconut milk, lemon juice, tofu, snow peas, and chili pepper. Cook for another minute or two. Serve with a sprinkling of coriander on top. *Serves 4 to 6*

Nutritional analysis per serving: 339 calories; 16.4 g fat (41.8% calories from fat); 4 mg cholesterol; 41.3 g carbohydrate; 10.1 g protein; 1710 mg sodium; 77 mg calcium; 4.4 mg iron; 38 mg vitamin C

---

*can be found in Asian, particularly Thai-Vietnamese markets, as well as in some health food stores

❀❀

GAZPACHO

This is the traditional cold soup of summer. Here I do not use oil or canned tomato juice.

5 large ripe tomatoes, chopped
2 small to medium cucumbers, chopped
1 small red onion, chopped
1 small red pepper, seeded and chopped
1 small green pepper, seeded and chopped
2 cloves garlic, minced
juice of a lemon
1 jalapeño pepper, seeded and sliced
1/4 cup chopped basil
1 sprig oregano

Reserve about 1/4 cup of the tomatoes, 1/2 of a cucumber, 2 tablespoons of onions and 2 tablespoons each of the peppers. Purée the rest of the ingredients in a blender until smooth. Pour into a large bowl and add the reserved chopped vegetables. Chill and serve.

Serves 4 to 6

Nutritional analysis per serving: 97 calories; 0.8 g fat (6.2% calories from fat); 0 mg cholesterol; 22.4 g carbohydrate; 3.9 g protein; 20 mg sodium; 76 mg calcium; 2.1 mg iron; 104 mg vitamin C

MISO SOUP

This is the traditional soup served at a Japanese meal and a macro-biotic favorite. Remember that miso is one of the rare vegetarian sources of vitamin B12.

> 6 cups water
> 1 4-inch piece kombu (dried kelp)
> 2 tablespoons dried bonito (optional: bonito is dried, flaked fish)
> 5 tablespoons miso
> 1/2 lb. tofu in 1-inch cubes
> 1 carrot, thinly sliced
> 2 scallions, thinly sliced
> 1 5-inch piece burdock root, peeled and thinly sliced (optional: usually found in health food stores)

Put the water in a pot and add the kombu. When the water boils, remove the kombu and reserve for later use. Add the bonito, turn off the heat, and let stand for a few minutes. Strain out the bonito. Add the carrot and burdock and cook until tender. Add the tofu. Mix the miso with water, add to the stock, and stir until mixed together. Add the scallions and serve.

> Serves 4 to 6

Nutritional analysis per serving: 77 calories; 2.7 g fat (29.9% calories from fat); 0 mg cholesterol; 9.0 g carbohydrate; 5.4 g protein; 533 mg sodium; 66 mg cal-cium; 2.8mg iron; 4 mg vitamin C

✿✿✿

PERSIAN SOY YOGURT SOUP

Redolent with herbs, with the crunch of the cucumbers and walnuts and the sweetness of the raisins, this is one of the most wonderful dishes I know.

1 quart soy yogurt
1 medium cucumber
1 small red onion
1 small leek or 3 scallions
1-2 tablespoons each fresh chopped dill, basil, tarragon,
*   mint, parsley*
1/2 cup raisins
1/4 cup chopped walnuts
petals from 2 rosehips (optional)

Chop all of the dry ingredients except the raisins. Add along with all other ingredients to the yogurt. The herbs, onions, and walnuts can be chopped in a food processor, but the cucumbers should be chopped by hand as they get too watery in a blender or processor. Sprinkle some raisins, walnuts, rose petals, and herbs on top.

Serves 4 to 6

Nutritional analysis per serving: 302 calories; 8.8 g fat (24.7% calories from fat); 0 mg cholesterol; 44.1 g carbohydrate; 15.9 g protein; 85 mg sodium; 166 mg calcium; 3.5 mg iron; 15 mg vitamin C

SORREL SOUP WITH ZUCCHINI

One summer, the zucchini grew to the size of the state of California and wild sorrel invaded the garden, so I made this soup to use some of the bounty. Any sorrel and zucchini will suffice for this fragrant soup.

2 large zucchini, chopped
2 cups sorrel
2 potatoes
2 cups vegetable stock, strained (see above)
1/2 cup fat-free soy milk
1/2 cup soy parmesan

Cook the potatoes in stock about 15 minutes. Add the zucchini and cook for 5 minutes more. Then add the sorrel and cook until wilted, just a minute or two. Purée all in a food processor, add the soy milk and soy parmesan, and stir.

Serves 4 to 6

Nutritional analysis per serving: 252 calories; 3.7 g fat (12.6% calories from fat); 1 mg cholesterol; 44.3 g carbohydrate; 12.9 g protein; 1091 mg sodium; 1489 mg calcium; 2.3 mg iron; 36 mg vitamin C

CABBAGE SOUP

Cabbage is one of the great antioxidants, resplendent with beta-carotene. So often thought of as an accompaniment to corned beef, it can make a meal in itself. This is one of the wonderful things you can do with it.

1 onion, sliced
6 garlic cloves, sliced
2 carrots, shredded
1 large potato, julienned
1 large turnip, julienned (optional)
1/2 head cabbage, shredded
6 cups water
2 bay leaves
1 teaspoon thyme
1 teaspoon sage
1 tablespoon oregano
4 tablespoons chopped parsley
4 tablespoons tomato paste
1 package fat-free soy Canadian bacon (optional, and found
    in health food stores)
sea salt and pepper to taste

Put the stock in a pot, bring to a boil, reduce heat, and add the other ingredients in order. Simmer for an hour.

Serves 4 to 6

Nutritional analysis per serving: 124 calories; 0.7 g fat (3.3% calories from fat); 0 mg cholesterol; 34.9 g carbohydrate; 9.4 g protein; 318 mg sodium; 156 mg calcium; 2.7 mg iron; 61 mg vitamin C

STEWS AND SIMMERED DISHES

CHICKPEA, JERUSALEM ARTICHOKE, AND CABBAGE *STEW*

This recipe is great for using an odd assortment of vegetables.

1/2 cup chickpeas, soaked in water for a day
2 cups vegetable stock or water
1 bay leaf
1 tablespoon thyme
1 onion, chopped
5 cloves garlic, chopped
1 lb. Jerusalem artichokes, cut in 1-inch pieces
2 carrots cut in 2-inch slices
1 large potato, cut in 8-10 pieces
1 teaspoon ground fennel seed
1 teaspoon cumin
pinch chili powder
1 teaspoon oregano
2 tomatoes, quartered
1/2 head green cabbage (or one small cabbage), sliced
1 package fat-free soy Canadian bacon (found in health food stores)

Cook the chickpeas in stock or water with the thyme and bay leaf for about an hour. Add the Jerusalem artichokes, carrots, potato, onions, garlic, and seasonings and cook until the vegetables are almost soft, about 20 minutes. Add the tomatoes and cabbage. Cut the soy bacon in 1-inch pieces and add. Cook for another 15 minutes. This is a hearty dish that can be served in a bowl—accompany with mustard.

Serves 4 to 6

Nutritional analysis per serving: 265 calories; 2.9 g fat (8.1% calories from fat); 1 mg cholesterol; 60.0 g carbohydrate; 14.5 g protein; 766 mg sodium; 126 mg calcium; 6.0 mg iron; 39 mg vitamin C

❧❧❧

CHICKPEAS WITH SPINACH

Another nutritious and delicious combination. The chickpeas supply protein. The spinach is rich in health-giving phytochemicals. Both the chickpeas and the spinach supply calcium and iron. Serve with brown rice and you have a complete protein.

1/2 cup chickpeas soaked in water
1 teaspoon mustard seeds
1 tablespoon cumin
1 teaspoon fenugreek
1 teaspoon turmeric
1 tablespoon coriander
1 tablespoon cinnamon
1 medium onion
4 cloves garlic
1-inch piece ginger
1 small chili or 1/4 teaspoon chili powder
1 cup water
1 lb. spinach, thoroughly washed and chopped
1 cup soy yogurt

Soak the chickpeas in water for a day and cook them in 1-1/2 cups water for about an hour. Meanwhile, put the mustard seeds in a skillet over moderate heat and cover. Cook until the seeds stop sputtering, a minute or two. Add the other spices and cook, stirring, until they begin to smoke lightly, giving off their aroma. Be careful not to let them burn. Chop the onion, garlic, ginger, and pepper in a food processor or spice grinder. This releases enough liquid to allow them to cook without any grease. Add to the spices, and keep stirring until soft. If the mixture begins to burn or to stick to the pan, add about 1/2 cup of water (which has to be added anyway after the onions are cooked). Add the cooked chickpeas and the washed and chopped spinach with stems removed. Mix thoroughly and cook, covered, over low heat until the spinach blends into the sauce. Add the soy yogurt and cook until blended and thick.

Serves 2 to 4

Nutritional analysis per serving: 254 calories; 5.8 g fat (19.2% calories from fat); 0 mg cholesterol; 39.7 g carbohydrate; 15.5 g protein; 127 mg sodium; 231 mg calcium; 8.0 mg iron37 mg vitamin C

WHITE BEANS WITH GREENS

Chard and kale are excellent cancer fighters, rich in carotenes and antioxidants and high in fiber. In this dish, the beans soften the greens, while the greens add pungency to the beans.

1/2 cup great northern, cannelli, or other white beans
1 bay leaf
1 tablespoon rosemary
1 teaspoon sage
1 onion, chopped
1 small leek, chopped
4 cloves garlic, chopped
1 bunch dill, chopped
1 bunch each of chopped kale, chard, spinach

Soak the beans in water overnight. Drain and put in a pot with 2 cups of fresh water, bay leaf, rosemary, and sage. Cook for about half an hour. Add the onions and garlic and cook until the beans soften, about a half hour more, then add the greens and the dill. Cook until the greens are wilted and soft and blend into the beans, about 15 minutes more. Add salt and pepper to taste.

Serves 4

Nutritional analysis per serving: 268 calories; 2.7 g fat (8.4% calories from fat); 0 mg cholesterol; 48.4 g carbohydrate; 17.8 g protein; 183 mg sodium; 403 mg calcium; 12.6 mg iron; 69 mg vitamin C

COUSCOUS WITH CHICKPEAS

This North African dish is usually prepared with meats. My adaptation is vegan, and I assure you that you won't miss the meat. The mix of the couscous with raisins and the vegetables with chickpeas is rich, filling, healthful, and delicious. Couscous is a grain and chickpeas are beans, so you have a complete protein.

1 cup couscous	*1 cup water*
1/2 cup chickpeas,	*2 carrots, sliced*
soaked in water for a day	*1 red and 1 yellow pepper,*
1/2 cup raisins	*cut into 1-inch pieces*
1 onion, sliced	*3 tablespoons cumin*
3 cloves garlic, chopped	*1 teaspoon saffron*
1 teaspoon olive oil	*1 teaspoon cinnamon*
1 zucchini, sliced	*2 tablespoons mint, chopped*

1 eggplant cut in slices and then quartered
4 tomatoes, quartered or 1 lb. canned tomatoes

Cook the chickpeas in boiling water until tender, about 1 hour. Sauté the onions and garlic in oil until soft. Add the spices and stir until they begin to let off their aroma. Add the tomatoes and cook until soft. Add the water and all the vegetables, including the chickpeas. Cook until the vegetables are soft, about 20 minutes. Top with mint. Meanwhile, put the couscous in boiling water, cook for a minute, turn off heat, and let it sit until the water is absorbed. Add the raisins. To serve, put a mound of couscous on a plate and surround it with the sauce.

Serves 4 to 6

Nutritional analysis per serving: 374 calories; 3.9 g fat (8.9% calories from fat); 0 mg cholesterol; 76.4 g carbohydrate; 13.2 g protein; 42 mg sodium; 124 mg calcium; 6.4 mg iron; 168 mg vitamin C

SQUASH STEW WITH COUSCOUS

This is a hearty, healthy stew that mixes a variety of flavors into a delicious dish.

1/2 cup dried black beans
1 medium winter squash (hubbard, butternut, etc.)
1 small red onion, chopped
5 cloves garlic, minced
four ripe tomatoes
small bunch of basil or oregano, chopped
pinch of cayenne
1 cup couscous
1/4 cup raisins or sun-dried tomatoes

Soak the black beans in water for at least 8 hours. Then cook for an hour until tender. Cut the squash into chunks, about 1-1/2 inches square, removing the seeds. Steam them until a fork can be put into them, 5 to 10 minutes, but don't let them get too soft. They will be cooked more later. Sauté the onions and garlic in a pot until soft. Cut the tomatoes into quarters and add to the pot. Then add the beans, squash, and seasonings and simmer for about ten minutes.

Meanwhile, boil one cup of water in a small saucepan and add the couscous. Cover, turn off the heat, and allow the water to be absorbed. When the couscous is fluffy, add the raisins or chopped sun-dried tomatoes. Put the couscous in the center of a platter or large bowl and surround it with the sauce.

Serves 4 to 6

Nutritional analysis per serving: 276 calories; 0.8 g fat (2.6% calories from fat); 0 mg cholesterol; 58.1 g carbohydrate; 10.8 g protein; 17 mg sodium; 59 mg calcium; 2.3 mg iron; 26 mg vitamin C

ALOO GOBI (POTATOES WITH CAULIFLOWER)

This Indian curry is a mix of vegetables, spices, and nuts. Cauliflower contains sulforaphane, a potent cancer fighter. There is some controversy over the chili pepper, but most reports give it high marks, not only as a cancer and heart disease preventative, but as a decongestant, too.

2 potatoes, chopped into 1-inch cubes
1 onion, chopped
4 cloves garlic, minced
2-inch piece ginger, minced
1 teaspoon canola oil
1/4 cup almonds, chopped
1 cup tomato puree or 3 ripe tomatoes
1/2 teaspoon chili
1 teaspoon turmeric
1 teaspoon coriander
1 teaspoon sea salt
1/2 teaspoon pepper
1 medium head cauliflower, broken into florets
2 teaspoons garam masala (recipe below)
1 cup water

Sauté the onions, garlic, and ginger in skillet. Add the almonds and all the spices except garam masala and sauté about 3 minutes. Add the tomatoes, potatoes, and cauliflower with 1 cup water and simmer until the vegetables are tender and the sauce is thick, about 15 to 20 minutes. Add the garam masala and serve.

continued

Garam masala can be found in Indian markets, but you can make
your own:

1 tablespoon cardamom

5 tablespoons coriander seeds

5 tablespoons cumin seeds

1 tablespoon whole cloves

4 tablespoons black peppers

1 4-inch piece cinnamon stick

4 bay leaves, crumbled

Heat a skillet over medium high heat and add all spices. Cook, stirring, until they turn brown. Be careful not to let them burn. Cool
and grind in a spice grinder or coffee mill.

Serves 4

Nutritional analysis per serving: 227 calories; 6.3 g fat (23.6% calories from
fat); 0 mg cholesterol; 39.0 g carbohydrate; 7.3 g protein; 277 mg sodium; 64
mg calcium; 2.3 mg iron; 73 mg vitamin C

SEMOLINA "RISOTTO" WITH VEGETABLES

This dish is simply seasoned, but rich with flavor.

1 teaspoon vegetable oil (light sesame or canola)
1/3 cup raw sliced almonds
1 tablespoon mustard seeds
1 red chili, chopped, seeds removed
5 chopped shallots or 1 large red onion
1-inch piece ginger, chopped
1 cup semolina
3 cups water
1 tablespoon cumin (optional)
1 tablespoon fenugreek (optional)
juice of 1/2 lemon
3 tablespoons chopped coriander

VEGETABLES:
1 large potato, cubed
1 medium eggplant, cubed
1 zucchini, cubed
2 carrots, sliced
1/2 cup peas, snow peas, or snap peas
1/2 lb. asparagus tips (optional)

Steam the potatoes for about 5 minutes. Add the eggplant, zucchini, and carrots and steam for another 5 minutes. The peas and asparagus require only a minute or two more. Sauté the almonds in oil until lightly browned. Remove and drain. Put the mustard seeds into the pan, cover, and cook over high heat until the sizzling stops. Add the shallots or onions and the ginger and sauté until lightly browned.

continued

Add the semolina and stir until coated. Add the water slowly, stirring as you pour. The semolina should be smooth and thick, but not lumpy. If too thick, add more water. Add the vegetables and keep stirring until well mixed and integrated with the semolina. I think that the dish is rich enough without the additional spices, but you could add them at this point, with the lemon juice and coriander, and stir all together. Put into a bowl and sprinkle with the almonds.

Serves 6

Nutritional analysis per serving: 257 calories; 6.4 g fat (2% calories from fat); 0 mg cholesterol; 43.4 g carbohydrate; 9.1 g protein; 63 mg sodium; 77 mg calcium; 3.8 mg iron; 46 mg vitamin C

RED LENTILS WITH YAMS AND CARROTS

This dish, made mostly of orange ingredients, can be thought of as beta-carotene stew. It is incredibly good to eat.

1 teaspoon cumin, ground
1 teaspoon coriander, ground
1 tablespoon turmeric
3/4 cup red lentils
1 small onion, chopped
2 cloves garlic, chopped
1-inch piece ginger, minced
1 large yam or sweet potato cut in 1-inch cubes
1 large carrot, sliced
1 cup water
1 cup cubed winter squash or pumpkin (optional)
1 cup cauliflower florets (optional)
1/4 cup grated coconut
sea salt
3 tablespoons chopped cilantro (optional)

Put the spices in a skillet and cook over low heat until they release their perfume. Add the onion, garlic, ginger, and red lentils and stir to coat. Add the vegetables and water and simmer for about 20 minutes or until the lentils are soft and the vegetables are cooked. Add the grated coconut, salt, and cilantro and stir for a few minutes.

Serves 4

Nutritional analysis per serving: 296 calories; 2.6 g fat (7.4% calories from fat); 0 mg cholesterol; 57.7 g carbohydrate; 14.5 g protein; 51 mg sodium; 91 mg calcium; 5.0 mg iron; 56 mg vitamin C

✿✿

RATATOUILLE

While this dish can be made all year round, it is great for end-of-summer, when all the vegetables can be picked from the garden or found at a farm stand.

1 medium eggplant, in 1/2-inch slices
1 red onion, sliced
1 teaspoon olive oil
5 cloves garlic, chopped
2 red or green peppers, in 1/2-inch julienne slices
2 medium zucchini, in 1/2-inch julienne slices
3 large ripe tomatoes, cut in 1/2-inch slices
1 sprig oregano, chopped
1 large sprig basil, leaves chopped
1 teaspoon sea salt

Grill the eggplant under the broiler or on a stovetop grill for about 5 minutes on each side, or until lightly browned. Remove from the oven and let cool. Slice into 1/2-inch julienne slices. Sauté the onion and garlic in olive oil and add the peppers, zucchini, and eggplant. Stir until they begin to soften and add the tomatoes. Cover and let simmer for about 10 minutes. Add the herbs and salt and cook for another minute or two.

Alternatively, put all ingredients in a clay pot that has been soaked in water for about 15 minutes and bake in a 350° oven until soft, 15 to 20 minutes. The clay pot cooks the vegetables without burning and without the need for oil.

Serves 2 to 4

Nutritional analysis per serving: 92 calories; 0.7 g fat (5.8% calories from fat); 0 mg cholesterol; 21.2 g carbohydrate; 3.7 g protein; 16 mg sodium; 58 mg calcium; 1.8 mg iron; 101 mg vitamin C

SEITAN WITH POMEGRANATE SAUCE

This dish is based on a Persian recipe for chicken with pomegranate sauce, one of the great dishes of Persian cuisine. To juice a pomegranate, roll it on a table or countertop with as much pressure as you can apply without breaking the skin. This releases the juice from the seeds. Then you can either make a small hole in the skin and squeeze the juice out or cut it in half and put it in a citrus juicer— preferably the kind with a lever that pulls a top down over the fruit. Pomegranates are red fruit, high in carotenes and vitamin C.

1 lb. seitan
sprinklng of herbs: thyme, sage, ground bay leaf
1 teaspoon canola oil (optional)
1 onion, finely chopped
2 cloves garlic, minced
2 tablespoons tomato purée or paste
1/2 cup chopped walnuts
1/2 teaspoon cinnamon
2 tablespoons lemon juice
1 cup fresh pomegranate juice or 2-3 tablespoons syrup
    (available at Middle Eastern markets)
1-2 cups water

Cut the seitan into 1/2-inch thick slices and sprinkle it with the ground herbs. Sauté the onion in a non-stick skillet (with or without the oil) until lightly browned and add the seitan. Add the tomato purée and stir together over low heat. While stirring, add the walnuts, cinnamon, lemon juice, and pomegranate juice, and continue to cook for 3 to 4 minutes. Add the water and cook for another 10 minutes. Serve with brown rice or Persian rice. *Serves 4*

Nutritional analysis per serving: 151 calories; 9.3 g fat (10.8% calories from fat); 0 mg cholesterol; 14.9 g carbohydrate; 159.1 g protein; 641 mg sodium; 34 mg calcium; 1.3 mg iron; 10 mg vitamin C

ENTRÉES

MAKING YOUR OWN PASTA

Many commercial pastas are freshly made, and while they taste delicious, they are invariably made with eggs. You can make your own pasta, but most health food stores carry a wide variety of pastas made with such ingredients as whole wheat, spelt, quinoa, and artichoke, and many are organic.

TO MAKE YOUR OWN PASTA:
3/4 cup whole wheat flour
1/4 cup semolina
1/4 cup water

Slowly add water to the flour on a pastry board, mixing with your hands until the dough is firm but not sticky. Knead about 8 minutes. Roll into about 5 balls and feed each into a pasta machine until it is thinned out (usually the sixth setting). Then cut to the desired width with an attachment (or use an automatic pasta machine).

For lasagne, roll to the 5th setting and do not cut the dough. For ravioli, cut dough into 2-inch squares, place filling in center of square, cover with second piece of dough and seal edges. There is a tool that will cut and seal the edges, giving the ravioli a decorative edge.

I have not specified which pasta for which sauce because I think it's really subject to taste.

Serves 2

LASAGNE WITH EGGPLANT

Most lasagne is made with ground beef. Eggplant is a meaty enough vegetable to make a truly satisfying and delicious substitute.

1 large eggplant	*1/4 cup soy parmesan*
1 red onion, chopped	*1 package lasagne*
5 cloves garlic, chopped	*parsley, chopped*
2 tablespoons of broth	*oregano, chopped*
* or tomato juice*	*sea salt*
3 large tomatoes, chopped	
1/2 lb. firm tofu	

1/4 lb. casein-free soy mozzarella, chopped or grated

Cut the eggplant into slices and sprinkle with salt. Let them sit for about half an hour or until they "sweat." Pat them dry and lightly bake or grill them (you can use a stovetop grill) until soft (about 4 minutes each side).

Sauté the onion and garlic in broth or tomato juice until transparent. Add the tomatoes and cook until soft. Crumble the tofu and add, stirring.

Cook the lasagne in water until soft but firm. Lightly oil a baking pan. Place a layer of lasagne on the bottom, with a layer of eggplant on top of it. Cover with half of the tomato-tofu mixture and a sprinkling of soy mozzarella and soy parmesan, herbs, and salt. If you can't find casein-free mozzarella, fix the tofu with miso instead, using 3/4 pound of tofu. Then place another layer of lasagne on top of that, repeat all other ingredients and a final layer of lasagne. Bake in a 350° oven for about 20 minutes. *Serves 4*

Variation: Lasagne with tomato and basil sauce.
Leave out the eggplant and substitute basil for oregano.

Nutritional analysis per serving: 776 calories; 124.9 g fat (44.1% calories from fat); 0 mg cholesterol; 185.6 g carbohydrate; 170.2 g protein; 590 mg sodium; 1456 mg calcium; 11.8 mg iron; 26 mg vitamin C

RAVIOLI WITH SPINACH

This is a great use for spinach, rich in beta-carotene, vitamin B6, folic acid, iron, and potassium.

1 bunch spinach
1 small onion, chopped
6 cloves garlic, chopped
1 teaspoon olive oil
1/4 lb. tofu
1/4 teaspoon ground nutmeg
1/3 cup chopped basil
1/4 cup soy parmesan
1 recipe pasta dough (see page 113)

Clean the spinach and steam for a minute or two until just wilted. Sauté the onion and garlic in olive oil and crumble in the tofu. Add the spinach and all the other ingredients except the soy parmesan. Stir all the ingredients together and purée in a food processor. Add the soy parmesan.

Place a tablespoon of the mixture on a 2-inch square of pasta dough. Place another piece on top and pinch edges together, with a pasta tool if you have one. Put the ravioli on a plate with semolina on it to prevent sticking. Repeat until all the dough is used.

Bring large pot of water to boil. Put ravioli into the pot, being careful not to crowd. Only put in enough for a single layer. When the ravioli has risen to the top of the water, let it cook for another minute, then remove with a slotted spoon. Repeat until all the ravioli is cooked. Serve with tomato sauce (see page 121).

Serves 2 to 4

continued

Nutritional analysis per serving: 393 calories; 6.0 g fat (13.5% calories from fat); 0 mg cholesterol; 66.5 g carbohydrate; 20.5 g protein; 266 mg sodium; 1139 mg calcium; 8.1 mg iron; 34 mg vitamin C

Variation: **Ravioli with Broccoli** is essentially the same as the spinach ravioli, but made with 2 to 3 stalks of broccoli. It is a great recipe for using broccoli stems. Peel the stems and cut them into 2-inch pieces. Steam for about 8 minutes. Then add the flowers and cook for another 5 minutes. Put the broccoli in the food processor before adding it to the onion-garlic mixture. You may also mix spinach and broccoli.

Variation: **Ravioli with Mushrooms and Red Pepper Sauce**
Mushrooms always turn a simple meal into a gourmet treat. Here is another way.

1 recipe pasta dough
1 recipe mushroom sauce, made with 1/4 cup soy milk
1 recipe red pepper sauce

Fill the ravioli with mushroom sauce and prepare as in the recipe for ravioli with spinach. Serve with red pepper sauce.

Serves 2 to 4

PENNE WITH "CHEESES" AND SAUCE

You might look at this dish as an upscale vegan macaroni and cheese. The cheeses are, of course, made from soy. Penne is a large cylindrical pasta. You could use other shapes instead.

1/3 pound penne
1 small red onion, chopped
5 cloves garlic, minced
1 tablespoon olive oil
1/4 pound mushrooms, sliced
2 large tomatoes, cut into 1/2-inch squares
1/3 pound soy mozzarella
4 tablespoons soy parmesan
1/4 cup chopped basil
1 tablespoon chopped oregano (optional)

Boil the penne in 2 cups of water until al dente. Sauté the onions and garlic in the olive oil until transparent. Add the sliced mushrooms and cook for another two minutes, stirring. Add the tomatoes and simmer until soft and moist. If the tomatoes aren't juicy enough, add a little water or tomato purée. Put the penne in a casserole dish and add the sauce. Chop the mozzarella and all but 1 tablespoon of the basil and stir in well. Sprinkle the top with the soy parmesan. Bake in a 350° oven for about 15 minutes. It should be bubbly, but not burned or dry. Add the rest of the basil and stir.

Serves 4

Nutritional analysis per serving: 810 calories; 335.2 g fat (54.2% calories from fat); 0 mg cholesterol; 235.0 g carbohydrate; 402.7 g protein; 1556 mg sodium; 4606 mg calcium; 8.7 mg iron; 61 mg vitamin C

POTATO GNOCCHI

Gnocchi are little dumplings made, in this recipe, from potatoes and served like pasta. These gnocchi are light and airy and can be served with many different sauces.

> *1-1/2 lbs. potatoes (not baking potatoes)*
> *1/2-1 cup whole wheat flour*
> *3 cups water or broth*

Boil the potatoes in their skins for half an hour or more, until soft all the way through. Peel and put through a strainer or food mill. A food processor will make them too mushy. Slowly add the flour, mixing with your hands. When the mixture is soft, pliant, and still a little sticky you've added enough flour. Knead for a few minutes. Roll into little balls, about 1 inch in diameter, and press your thumb into one side to make an indentation.

Fill a large pot with broth or salted water (the broth will give the gnocci an enhanced flavor) and bring to a boil. Put in enough balls to make a layer and cook, over moderate heat, until after they rise to the top, about 20 seconds. Remove with a slotted spoon and put in a bowl. Continue until all are cooked. Serve with tomato-basil sauce or pesto sauce.

> *Serves 4 to 6*

Nutritional analysis per serving: 177 calories; 0.5 g fat (2.7% calories from fat); 0 mg cholesterol 39.3 g carbohydrate;5.7 g protein; 9 mg sodium; 17 mg calcium; 1.8 mg iron; 25 mg vitamin C

SPINACH GNOCCHI

Spinach gnocchi are dumplings minus the potato. These dumplings are full of nutrients. If you can't eat wheat, substitute another type of flour.

1 lb. spinach
2 shallots, minced
1 teaspoon olive oil
1/2 lb. tofu
1/2 cup whole wheat flour
1/4 teaspoon nutmeg
1 heaping tablespoon egg replacer in 2 tablespoons water
1/2 cup soy parmesan

Wash and lightly steam the spinach. Sauté the shallots in olive oil until light brown (or roast them, avoiding the oil). Put the shallots, spinach, and tofu in a food processor and chop. Transfer these ingredients to a bowl and slowly add the flour and egg replacer (stirred into water until it is blended), mixing with hands until the mixture feels smooth. Add the nutmeg and the soy parmesan. Form dough into small balls, 1 inch or less in diameter.

Bring salt water to boil in a pot and put in a layer of gnocchi. Cook over moderate heat until they rise to the surface. Remove with a slotted spoon. Serve with red pepper sauce, plain tomato sauce (see page 121) or tomato sauce with red pepper purée. You can add parsley and/or basil to the food processor when you mix the tofu and spinach.

Serves 2 to 4

Nutritional analysis per serving: 234 calories; 8.0 g fat (27.7% calories from fat); 0 mg cholesterol; 26.4 g carbohydrate; 20.3 g protein; 434 mg sodium; 2120 mg calcium; 8.0 mg iron; 32 mg vitamin C

PESTO SAUCE

Basil is rich in monoterpenes, which protect against cancer and heart disease. Pesto is typically made with a lot of olive oil. Here are several options:

> 2 cups basil
> 3 tablespoons olive oil
> 5-6 cloves garlic
> 1/2 cup casein-free soy parmesan
> sea salt to taste

Blend all ingredients in a food processor. Put into a bowl, add pasta, toss, and serve.

Variations:

With tomato: Finely chop two tomatoes. Omit the oil and add about 4 heaping tablespoons to the blender. Put the rest of the tomato into a bowl, mix into the sauce, add pasta, toss, and serve.

With zucchini: Chop a zucchini into small cubes. Sauté lightly in 1 tablespoon of olive oil until light brown. Add to the sauce.

With broccoli: Steam about a cup of broccoli flowers for a few minutes. Add to the sauce.

Serves 2 to 4

Nutritional analysis per serving: 131 calories; 8.7 g fat (55.5% calories from fat); 0 mg cholesterol; 7.6 g carbohydrate; 8.1 g protein; 259 mg sodium; 1564 mg calcium; 2.5mg iron; 15 mg vitamin C

❀❀❀

TOMATO SAUCE

Tomatoes have a bad reputation as a member of the nightshade family. In my experience, the only real negative of nightshades is that they exacerbate arthritis. Those who suffer seriously from arthritis might want to cut down on tomatoes, but for the rest of us, they are wonderful medicine. Tomatoes are rich in vitamin C and lycopenes, both of which fight cancer, especially prostate cancer. So the good news is much better than the bad news.

1 red onion
4 cloves garlic
1 tablespoon olive oil
4 large ripe tomatoes, chopped, or 2 cups canned tomatoes
1 bunch of basil
sea salt

Chop the onions and garlic and sauté in olive oil until light brown. Add the salt and tomatoes and simmer lightly in their own juice, covered, about 10 to 15 minutes. Chop the basil and cook for only about a minute more. Alternatively, cook the onions and garlic in the tomato sauce without first sautéing them in the oil.

Serves 2 to 4

Nutritional analysis per serving: 114 calories; 4.9 g fat (35.5% calories from fat); 0 mg cholesterol; 17.6 g carbohydrate; 2.5 g protein; 19 mg sodium; 55 mg calcium; 1.6 mg iron; 40 mg vitamin C

ROASTED RED AND YELLOW PEPPER SAUCE

The sweet-tart flavor of the roasted red or yellow pepper is great in sauces. Red and yellow peppers contain lycopenes, which fight cancer, as well as vitamins A and C—even more than oranges—so they are nutritious as well as delicious.

2 red peppers
2 yellow peppers
5 cloves garlic
1 teaspoon olive oil
sea salt
1 sprig basil
casein-free soy parmesan

Grill the peppers until charred all over. When cool enough to handle, remove the skin, holding the peppers over a bowl to catch their liquid. Cut them in half, releasing the liquid into the bowl. Discard the seeds, ribs, and stems and slice thinly. Sauté the garlic in olive oil and add peppers, their liquid, and salt. Chop and add basil and cook for only about a minute more. Add to pasta and sprinkle with soy parmesan.

Variation:
Soak sun-dried tomatoes in water and slice when soft. Add to the sauce with the roasted peppers.
  Serves 2 to 4

Nutritional analysis per serving: 103 calories; 1.5 g fat (11.8% calories from fat); 0 mg cholesterol; 19.0 g carbohydrate; 6.7 g protein; 176 mg sodium; 994 mg calcium; 1.2 mg iron; 454 mg vitamin C

RED BEAN SAUCE

Pasta is a wonderful base for a vegan meal, but too much of it would leave you low on protein. This is an unexpectedly wonderful way of mixing protein-rich beans into a pasta dish. For variety, add a chopped tomato to the sauce, along with the beans.

1 cup red kidney beans
1 red onion, minced
4 cloves garlic, minced
2 cups broth
2 tablespoons chopped oregano

Soak the beans in water for a day. Sauté the onions and garlic in 2 tablespoons of broth until transparent. Add the beans and the rest of the broth and cook until beans are soft, about an hour. Add the oregano and cook for a few minutes more. Purée in a food processor. Add to pasta, toss, and serve.

Serves 2 to 4

Nutritional analysis per serving: 348 calories; 3.5 g fat (8.8% calories from fat); 2 mg cholesterol; 61.9 g carbohydrate; 19.6 g protein; 1119 mg sodium; 174 mg calcium; 7.8 mg iron; 10 mg vitamin C

EGGPLANT SAUCE

Eggplant can be very bitter if not cooked properly. Roasting takes away the bitterness and makes the eggplant creamy.

Eggplant is rich in certain phytochemicals, such as terpenes, which fight some tumors and have antioxidant properties. Eggplant is also good for the heart, with low fat and calories.

1 large eggplant or two Japanese eggplants
1 red onion
4 cloves garlic
2 large tomatoes, chopped
1 sprig basil or 2 of oregano
sea salt
casein-free soy parmesan

Grill the eggplant over an open flame on a gas stove or under an electric broiler (see "Spicy Eggplant" on page 185 in "Vegetables as Side Dishes"). They char quickly, so keep turning them every couple of minutes. When charred all over and soft to the touch on all sides, including the ends, remove from the heat and cool. Skin the eggplant and mash the meat. Roast the onions and the garlic in a 400° oven until soft but not burned, turning every few minutes, then chop. Put the onions, garlic, eggplant, and tomatoes into a pot and simmer until the tomatoes are nearly liquid. Add the herbs and sea salt and cook for a minute or two more. Toss with the pasta and serve with the soy parmesan.

Serves 2 to 4

Nutritional analysis per serving: 95 calories; 1.6 g fat (13.7% calories from fat); 0 mg cholesterol; 15.5 g carbohydrate; 7.2 g protein; 218 mg sodium; 1233 mg calcium; 0.7 mg iron; 7 mg vitamin C

❀❀❀❀❀❀❀❀❀❀❀❀❀❀❀❀❀❀❀❀❀❀❀❀❀❀❀❀❀❀❀❀❀❀❀❀❀❀

MUSHROOM SAUCE

1 small onion

3 cloves garlic

1 pound mushrooms, sliced (use a variety: porcini, cremini, white, oyster, if available)

1/2 cup fat-free soy milk

1 tablespoon arrowroot

3 tablespoons chopped parsley

2 tablespoons chopped tarragon

Sauté the onion and garlic in 2 tablespoons of soy milk until transparent. Add the mushrooms and cook until tender. Add the rest of the soy milk with arrowroot dissolved in it. Stir until thickened. If not thick enough, add a little more arrowroot. If too thick, add a little more milk. Add the herbs and salt. Cook just a minute more. Serve on pasta or use on or in crepes.

Serves 2 to 4

Nutritional analysis per serving: 92 calories; 0.9 g fat (8.1% calories from fat); 0 mg cholesterol; 18.6 g carbohydrate; 5.1 g protein; 11 mg sodium; 78 mg calcium; 3.2 mg iron; 12 mg vitamin C

BROCCOLI SAUCE

As broccoli is one of the most healthful foods you can eat, I always look for another way to use it. Pasta and broccoli are a great combination.

2 heads broccoli
2 tablespoons broth
5 garlic cloves, minced
2 large sprigs fresh oregano, chopped
juice of 1 lemon
1/4 cup soy parmesan
pepper

Separate the broccoli into florets. Peel one or two stems, depending on their thickness, and cut them into a thin julienne. Steam for about 5 minutes. Sauté the garlic lightly in the broth. Add the broccoli and stir. Add the oregano and lemon juice and stir until well covered, then grind some pepper over the mixture. Put the pasta in a bowl and add the sauce with the soy parmesan on top. Stir and serve. Broccoli rabe may be used instead of regular broccoli.

Serves 2 to 4

Nutritional analysis per serving: 154 calories; 3.3g fat (17.7% calories from fat); 1 mg cholesterol; 25.0 g carbohydrate; 9.9 g protein; 985 mg sodium; 835 mg calcium; 3.0 mg iron; 118 mg vitamin C

PUTANESCA SAUCE

The capers and olives give this dish a heady flavor, but they are *not* for the faint of palate.

8 *plum or 4 regular, very ripe tomatoes, chopped*
6 *sun-dried tomatoes, soaked in water until soft*
1 *medium red onion, chopped*
5 *cloves garlic, minced*
1 *tablespoon olive oil*
3 *tablespoons capers*
1/2 *cup pitted black olives, chopped*

Sauté the onions and garlic in olive oil until golden brown. Add the rest of the ingredients and simmer for about a half hour.

Serves 2 to 4

Nutritional analysis per serving: 465 calories; 10.8 g fat (18.1% calories from fat); 0 mg cholesterol; 90.2 g carbohydrate; 19.4 g protein; 2572 mg sodium; 174 mg calcium; 12.4 mg iron; 116 mg vitamin C

RICE DISHES

RISOTTO PRIMAVERA

A perfect risotto depends on the way it is cooked. The heat must be medium low. If it is too low, the liquid will not absorb quickly enough; too high and the risotto will burn or the liquid will evaporate too quickly. The right balance gives the right consistency.

In addition to the vegetables listed below, you could use string-beans, broccoli, peas, artichoke hearts, and sun-dried tomatoes. Risotto is usually made with chicken stock, so when you order it in a restaurant, be sure to ask.

1 leek, chopped	*1/2 cup snow or snap peas*
3 cloves garlic, chopped	*1/2 lb. asparagus*
1 teaspoon olive oil	*1 small zucchini, chopped*
1 cup arborio rice	*2 tomatoes, chopped*
6 cups vegetable broth	*1/2 cup dill, chopped*
1/2 lb. mushrooms, sliced	*1/2 cup basil, chopped*
1 red pepper, seeded and	*1/4 cup casein-free soy parmesan*
* cut into 1-inch pieces*	

Sauté the onions and garlic in oil until soft. Add the rice and stir until coated. Slowly add the broth, one ladle at a time, stirring each time until liquid is absorbed. When the rice is about cooked, add the vegetables, saving the peas and basil for last. Continue adding broth until the rice and vegetables are cooked. Add soy parmesan and serve.

Serves 4

Nutritional analysis per serving: 505 calories; 7.4 g fat (12.9% calories from fat); 4 mg cholesterol; 91.8 g carbohydrate; 20.0 g protein; 2679 mg sodium; 923 mg calcium; 8.0 mg iron; 63 mg vitamin C

RISOTTO WITH MUSHROOMS

This is a great treat to make for a special dinner.

1 leek or 4 scallions, chopped

3 cloves garlic, chopped

1 teaspoon olive oil

1 lb. white mushrooms, sliced

1/2 lb. porcini, cremini, chanterelle, or other wild
  mushrooms, chopped

1 cup arborio rice

6 cups vegetable stock with mushrooms

4 tablespoons fresh tarragon, chopped

1/2 teaspoon nutmeg

1/2 cup casein-free soy parmesan

Sauté the leeks and garlic in oil until soft. Add the mushrooms and stir briefly. Add the rice and stir to coat. Slowly add the stock, one ladle at a time, allowing the water to be absorbed before adding the next ladle. When the rice is cooked, add the tarragon and nutmeg and stir for another minute. Add the soy parmesan and serve.

Serves 4

Nutritional analysis per serving: 682 calories; 8.9 g fat (11.1% calories from fat); 4 mg cholesterol; 132.8 g carbohydrate; 27.5 g protein; 2760 mg sodium; 1571 mg calcium; 7.2 mg iron; 15 mg vitamin C

COCONUT RICE

You can use either white or brown basmati rice. The white rice is not bleached, but the husk is removed, so it has fewer vitamins than the brown rice. The white rice has a slightly more delicate taste. The added coconut milk gives the dish a richer flavor. However, coconut is one of the few non-meat products that has saturated fats, so use it sparingly.

1/2 cup water
1/2 cup coconut milk
1 cup basmati rice
8 cardamom pods
2 tablespoons grated unsweetened coconut (optional)

Boil the water and coconut milk, reduce the heat, and add the other ingredients. Cook until the rice is soft. Brown rice takes longer to cook than white basmati rice.

Serves 4

Nutritional analysis per serving: 239 calories; 9.2 g fat (34.2% calories from fat); 0 mg cholesterol; 35.0 g carbohydrate; 4.8 g protein; 42 mg sodium; 6 mg calcium; 2.3 mg iron; 1 mg vitamin C

RICE WITH SHITAKE MUSHROOMS AND TREE EARS

This Chinese rice dish is rich with beneficial foods garlic, ginger, shitake mushrooms, and tree ears, all of which fight cancer and help the heart.

1/2 cup brown rice
3/4 cup water
4 scallions or 1 small leek, chopped
4 cloves garlic, chopped
1 tablespoon ginger, chopped
1 teaspoon oil
6 shitake mushrooms, soaked in water until soft
   (or fresh shitakes)
3 tree ears, soaked in water until soft
2 tablespoons soy sauce
1 tablespoon rice wine (optional)
1/4 teaspoon four-spices powder

Cook the rice in water until soft. Sauté the scallions, ginger, and garlic in oil until soft and just turning brown. Add the mushrooms, tree ears, and soy sauce (and optional rice wine) and stir for a minute. Add the rice and five-spices powder, mix all the ingredients together, cook for another minute, and serve.

Serves 4

Nutritional analysis per serving: 218 calories; 2.5 g fat (10.5% calories from fat); 0 mg cholesterol; 43.5 g carbohydrate; 5.1 g protein; 521 mg sodium; 37 mg calcium; 1.5 mg iron; 5 mg vitamin C

LENTILS AND RICE

Few recipes have the basic mix of vegetarian beans and rice. This one gives the right balance of amino acids to form a protein that is as complete as any that you would get in meat.

1 medium onion, chopped
4 cloves garlic, chopped
1 teaspoon olive oil
1 cup brown rice
1/2 cup lentils
1 teaspoon cumin
1/2 teaspoon cinnamon
1 teaspoon cloves
5 cardamom pods or 1/4 teaspoon cardamom powder
2 cups water
1/4 cup raisins
1/4 cup chopped walnuts or slivered almonds

Sauté the onions and garlic in olive oil until soft. Add the rice, lentils, and spices and stir to coat. Add the water and bring to a boil, then lower the heat and cook 20 to 30 minutes. Add the raisins and nuts, cook for another minute, and serve.

Serves 4

Nutritional analysis per serving: 313 calories; 2.8 g fat (7.9% calories from fat); 0 mg cholesterol; 61.9 g carbohydrate; 11.8 g protein; 8 mg sodium; 54 mg calcium; 3.8 mg iron; 5 mg vitamin C

SAFFRON RICE

Paella is a Spanish rice dish with poultry, sausages, fish, shellfish, and vegetables. This dish shows off what is left if you make the paella only with vegetables.

1 large onion, chopped
1 teaspoon olive oil
4 cloves garlic, minced
1 cup brown basmati rice
1 medium sized zucchini cut into small cubes, about 1/4-inch
3 tomatoes, chopped
1 red and one yellow pepper, cut into 1/2-inch pieces
2 cups vegetable stock
1 teaspoon saffron threads
1/2 cup shelled peas or 1/4 lb. sugar snap peas
1/4 cup chopped basil leaves

Sauté the onions in a casserole pan for a few minutes until golden, then add the garlic. Stir for a minute, then add the rice and continue stirring until the rice is coated. Add the zucchini, tomatoes, and the peppers and stir for another minute or two. Then add the stock and the saffron and slowly bring to a boil. Simmer until the water is absorbed, about 15 to 20 minutes. The timing depends on the kind of rice you use. Basmati rice usually takes slightly less time than regular brown rice. Add the peas and basil and cook for another minute or two. Add salt and pepper to taste and serve.

Serves 4

Nutritional analysis per serving: 398 calories; 5.2 g fat (11.2% calories from fat); 1 mg cholesterol; 80.4 g carbohydrate; 11.8 g protein; 858 mg sodium; 81 mg calcium; 4.1 mg iron; 238 mg vitamin C

BROWN RICE WITH VEGETABLES

Most health food restaurants offer the standard macrobiotic dish of steamed rice with vegetables. The simplest recipe is actually the best. There are those who believe that a diet of brown rice and steamed vegetables is all that a person with cancer should eat if a total cure is desired. I'm not sure that I entirely agree with that point of view as there are other foods that fight cancer and are necessary for complete nutrition. What is more, everything in this book serves that purpose. However, here is a 100% nutritionally correct, macrobiotically acceptable recipe.

1 cup brown rice
1 bunch broccoli
1 bunch spinach, kale, chard, or other greens
3 pieces bok choy
2 carrots
1 squash, summer or winter
1/2 lb. tofu, cubed
1/4 lb. snow or snap peas
1 small onion
5 tablespoons stock
2 cloves garlic
1-inch piece of ginger
2 tablespoons tamari soy sauce
1 tablespoon arrowroot or kudzu
2 tablespoons sesame seeds

Cook the brown rice in two cups of water until the water is absorbed and the rice is soft, about 20 minutes. Cut the carrots, bok choy, and squash into slices about 1/4-inch thick. Wash and dry the greens and chop lightly. Cut the broccoli into florets and string the peas.

continued

Steam the vegetables in a large steaming pot in the following order: First the carrots for about 5 minutes, then add the bok choy, broccoli, and squash for another 5 minutes. Add the greens, tofu, and peas and cook until greens are wilted.

Chop the onions and mince the garlic and ginger. Sauté the onions in broth for a few minutes, until just lightly browned, and add the garlic and ginger. Stir for another minute and add the tamari. Dissolve the arrowroot or kudzu in 3 tablespoons of water and add to the pan. Stir until lightly thickened. Put all the vegetables and rice on a plate and pour the sauce over the vegetables.

Serves 4

Nutritional analysis per serving: 371 calories; 7.6 g fat (17.2% calories from fat); 0 mg cholesterol; 63.2 g carbohydrate; 18.5 g protein; 858 mg sodium; 349 mg calcium; 9.4 mg iron; 176 mg vitamin C

WRAPPED DISHES

When you don't have a solid piece of meat on your plate, you try to find ways to make food that satisfies your hunger. These wrapped dishes are delightful, filling meals all by themselves.

SPINACH PIE

A Greek spinach pie, or spanakopita, is made with feta cheese. If you eat cheese, feta is a good choice because goats are usually raised in a healthier way than cattle. However, tofu and soy parmesan are just as good as feta. This is a lighter and healthier recipe than the Greek version, which is made with more oil.

STUFFING:
1 lb. spinach
2 leeks or 6 scallions
4 cloves garlic
1 teaspoon olive oil
1/2 lb. tofu, crumbled
1/4 teaspoon ground nutmeg
1/4 cup chopped dill
1/2 cup soy milk
1 tablespoon arrowroot
1/4 cup soy parmesan

Thoroughly wash the spinach and steam it until just wilted, 3 to 4 minutes. Chop. In a skillet, sauté the leek or onion and garlic until soft and golden. Add the chopped spinach and stir. Add the tofu, nutmeg, and dill. Dissolve the arrowroot in the soy milk and add to skillet. Stir until it begins to thicken. Add soy parmesan.

PHYLLO PASTRY:

Phyllo is sold in gourmet shops and Middle Eastern groceries in boxes of 20 or so sheets. They are usually in the freezer compartment. Most of the time, they are made with bleached flour and preservatives. If you want whole wheat, organic, preservative-free phyllo, you'll probably have to make it yourself. Making dough as thin as commercially-made phyllo is the tricky part, and you can try it with a rolling pin on a floured board. However, I have had great success using a manual pasta machine and rolling through the thinnest setting. It will be narrower dough than the commercial variety, but adequate for this dish.

1 cup whole wheat pastry flour
1 teaspoon olive oil
pinch of sea salt
water

Sieve the flour and salt and add the oil. Slowly add just enough water to keep the dough together. Knead until soft. Slightly oil a bread or paté pan and add a piece of phyllo. Lightly brush with oil and put another piece on top. Repeat with 3 or 4 pieces. Add half the spinach mix and another layer of 3 to 4 pieces of phyllo. Then add the rest of the spinach and put 3 to 4 more pieces of lightly oiled phyllo on top. Bake in a 350° oven for 15 to 20 minutes.

Serves 4 to 6

Nutritional analysis per serving: 246 calories; 6.8 g fat (23.1% calories from fat); 0 mg cholesterol; 35.7 g carbohydrate; 15.6 g protein; 210 mg sodium; 960 mg calcium; 8.6 mg iron; 28 mg vitamin C

VEGETABLE PHYLLO PIE

2-3 red peppers
1 eggplant, sliced
2 zucchini, sliced
1 red onion, sliced
2 tomatoes
1 lb. spinach
6 sheets phyllo made with whole wheat pastry flour
    (see spinach pie recipe)
1 large sprig basil
1 sprig rosemary (optional)
1 teaspoon olive oil
salt to taste

Grill the red peppers, turning as each side chars. Remove the skins and the seeds. Slice the eggplant, zucchini, onion, and tomatoes into 1/4-inch rounds and grill lightly until soft and lightly browned. This should take about 4 minutes per side. Wash the spinach free of all grit and steam it until it just starts to wilt. Slice the tomatoes in 1/4-inch slices.

Place 3 or 4 pieces of phyllo in the bottom of a non-stick baking pan and lightly brush them with olive oil. Place a layer of eggplant, then zucchini, then tomato, then onion and basil on top, then add another 3 sheets of phyllo. Repeat layering of all the vegetables, finishing this time with the spinach on top. Cover with 3 or 4 layers of phyllo and bake in a 350° oven for 15 to 20 minutes. Cut it into 4 to 6 squares and serve. Meanwhile, make the sauce.

SAUCE:
1/2 cup vegetable stock
1 russet potato
2 roasted red peppers, peeled

Cook the potato in water or stock, then blend it with the pepper in a food processor. Slowly add the stock until the consistency is smooth and moist, but not too thin. (Only a Russet potato gives the consistency needed for the sauce. If you can't find any, use 1 table-spoon of arrowroot dissolved in water instead.) Put the stock and puréed pepper in a saucepan over low heat and add arrowroot. Whisk until thickened and smooth. You could also just purée the peppers and use that as sauce. Put each serving on a plate and sur-round with sauce.

Serves 4 to 6

Nutritional analysis per serving: 197 calories; 3.8g fat (16.1% calories from fat); 0 mg cholesterol; 37.0 g carbohydrate; 7.7 g protein; 216 mg sodium; 135 mg calcium; 4.7 mg iron; 152 mg vitamin C

BURRITO

Every health food restaurant seems to have a burrito on its menu. That is because combining beans and rice, which together have complementary amino acids, is a standard method of raising the value of the protein. Some nutritionists feel the beans and rice must be consumed together to get complete protein. Others feel that consuming enough complementary amino acids from different sources over the course of a day or two is sufficient.

1 small onion, chopped
1 jalapeño, chopped
4 cloves garlic, chopped
1 tablespoon olive oil
1 cup cooked kidney beans
4 tortillas
1/2 cup cooked brown rice
1 avocado, sliced
1 tomato, diced
1 small cucumber, chopped
1/4 lb. casein-free soy Monterey jack or mozzarella
1 cup lettuce, shredded
4 tablespoons chopped cilantro

Sauté the onions, jalapeño, and garlic in olive oil. Add the beans and stir for a minute. Put the bean mixture into a food processor and blend until smooth. Put the tortillas in a skillet with the soy cheese on top to one side. Cook over low heat until the cheese melts, being careful not to burn the tortilla. (This can also be done under a broiler.)

Put the tortillas on a plate. Put 2 heaping tablespoons of the beans over the cheese, add 2 tablespoons of rice, a few slices of avocado, a tablespoon of the tomato, 1 tablespoon of cucumber, a bit of the shredded lettuce, and a sprinkling of the cilantro. Fold in the sides of the tortilla and roll it up.

Serves 4

Nutritional analysis per serving: 330 calories; 71.4 g fat (52.4% calories from fat); 0 mg cholesterol; 66.4 g carbohydrate; 79.2 g protein; 369 mg sodium; 407 mg calcium; 4.2 mg iron; 37 mg vitamin C

FISH-FREE SUSHI

Sushi is one of those dishes you think you cannot possibly make at home. It is, however, much easier than you think. What is more, the sushi in most restaurants is made with bleached rice, so you are safer making it at home with an organic sushi rice or with brown rice. Personally, I don't favor using brown rice, as it must be made in a pressure cooker to be sticky enough to use in sushi. This recipe uses an organic sushi rice.

Sesame seeds and seaweed are much richer in calcium than milk, so this is a wonderful dish if you are on a dairy-free diet. Nori is not as high in calcium and iron as some other seaweeds, but it is an excellent source of vitamin A.

1 cup sushi rice
1-inch piece kombu
4 tablespoons rice vinegar (or make a mix of rice and
 umeboshi vinegars)
1 tablespoon sucanat
1 small cucumber
1 carrot, blanched
1 avocado
1 scallion
4 sheets nori seaweed
sesame seeds
1-2 tablespoons wasabi (Japanese horseradish)
4 tablespoons pickled ginger
light soy sauce
1/4 cup shredded daikon (white radish)

Put 1 to 2 tablespoons of wasabi in a small bowl and add 1 tablespoon of warm water. Mix together and let sit for at least 1/2 hour. Cook the rice in 2 cups of water with kombu buried in it. Remove the kombu once the rice boils. Cook on high heat for a minute, then cover and lower heat for about 10 minutes. When the rice is sticky and soft and the water almost gone, raise the heat for a few seconds. Put the rice into a wooden bowl and smooth it out with a wooden spoon. Dissolve the sucanat in vinegar over low heat, then pour it on top of the rice and smooth it into the rice. Cover the bowl with a damp cloth and let it sit while you prepare the vegetables.

You can use a variety of vegetables for sushi. Use them individually or mixed together as in a California roll. Slice the cucumbers, carrots, avocado, and scallions into 1/8-inch julienne strips. Put a sheet of nori on a bamboo mat. With a wooden spoon, cover the nori with rice, smoothing it down thinly. Sprinkle all over with sesame seeds. Add one or more vegetables at one end and roll, pushing with the mat to form a tight roll. Put the roll aside on a plate covered with a towel until all are done. When ready to serve, slice the roll into 1- to 2-inch pieces.

Serve by putting slices of sushi on a wooden board with the wasabi, daikon, and ginger. Put soy sauce in little bowls. Each person should have his or her own bowl and put as much wasabi as desired into it. Add soy sauce. Dip the sushi into the sauce with ginger, if desired.

Variations: You can also use sliced shitake mushrooms, pickled daikon and other pickled vegetables, tofu, spinach, dried gourd, or virtually any other vegetable in sushi. Be careful about buying prepared sushi vegetables in a Japanese market. They are often filled with MSG or other chemicals.

Serves 2 to 4

Nutritional analysis per serving: 355 calories; 10.6 g fat (26.6% calories from fat); 0 mg cholesterol; 57.3 g carbohydrate; 8.9 g protein; 1056 mg sodium; 151 mg calcium; 5.2 mg iron; 38 mg vitamin C

STUFFED RICE PAPERS WITH CURRY SAUCE

This recipe is filled with the health-giving ingredients shitake, garlic, and tree ears.

1 small onion, sliced
3 cloves garlic, minced
1 teaspoon canola oil
4 rice paper skins
8 shitake mushrooms, soaked and sliced thin
2-3 tree ears, soaked and sliced thin
1 oz. bean thread noodles, soaked and chopped
About 10 water chestnuts, cooked, peeled, and sliced
  (or canned)

Sauté the onions and garlic in oil and add the rest of the ingredients. Simmer for a few minutes. Add the arrowroot in water and stir until thickened. Soften the rice papers by brushing water on both sides. When soft, put 1/4 of the mixture into each one and roll it, folding the sides. Place in a baking dish with a little water on bottom. Bake at 350° for 15 minutes. Meanwhile, make the curry sauce.

CURRY SAUCE:
1 teaspoon canola oil
1 small onion, minced
3 garlic cloves, minced
1 tablespoon minced ginger
1 teaspoon ground cumin
1/2 teaspoon ground coriander
1 teaspoon ground turmeric
1/4 teaspoon ground fenugreek
1/4 teaspoon chili power
1 cup thick coconut milk

Sauté the onions in oil until soft. Add the garlic and stir for another minute. Blend in the spices, then add the coconut and mix until smooth. Cook until thickened. If too watery, add a teaspoon of arrowroot dissolved in water and cook until thickened. To serve, place a stuffed rice paper on a plate and cover with curry sauce.

Variation: Use phyllo instead of rice papers. Fold over a piece of phyllo and put the stuffing in the center. Bring up the corners into a sort of a purse-like shape and tie with a scallion green.

Serves 4

Nutritional analysis per serving: 305 calories; 17.2 g fat (48.4% calories from fat); 0 mg cholesterol; 36.2 g carbohydrate; 5.1 g protein; 147 mg sodium; 45 mg calcium; 1.9 mg iron; 9 mg vitamin C

CHICKPEA CREPES WITH SPINACH STUFFING AND MUSHROOM SAUCE

This dish uses an Indian recipe for the crepes and my own recipes for the stuffing and sauce. While the latter are not Indian at all, they blend beautifully. The crepes are made with chickpea flour, which works much better than other flours for making a flat pancake. It is also a bean flour, high in protein, calcium, and iron.

SPINACH STUFFING:
1 lb. spinach, cleaned and steamed
1 leek, the white part and 1/2 the green
3 cloves garlic
4 tablespoons chopped dill
1-2 tablespoons chopped parsley
2 tablespoons vegetable broth or water
4 tablespoons soy parmesan
   (optional: use if not using ginger in crepe)
1 tablespoon arrowroot in 1 tablespoon water

Chop the leek, then sauté it in oil until soft. Add the garlic and stir for a few seconds. Add the spinach, dill, parsley, and broth, and stir together. Add the arrowroot in water and stir until thickened. Add the soy parmesan (optional).

CREPES:
1 cup chickpea flour
1 cup water
1 teaspoon canola oil
1 teaspoon salt
1 tablespoon chopped ginger (optional)

Mix all the ingredients until smooth. You can use a food processor. Put a thin coat of oil in a non-stick crepe pan and add enough batter to thinly cover the pan. Cook over medium heat for about 2 minutes, or until the bottom starts to brown. Turn with a spatula and cook for another minute. Remove to a plate and repeat until the batter is used. Put about 2 heaping tablespoons of spinach filling in each crepe, fold the sides over, and roll it up. Cover with Mushroom Sauce and serve (see page 125).

Serves 2 to 4

Nutritional analysis per serving: 356 calories; 7.4 g fat (17.6% calories from fat); 0 mg cholesterol; 55.9 g carbohydrate; 21.6 g protein; 355 mg sodium; 1233 mg calcium; 9.8 mg iron; 40 mg vitamin C

STUFFED VEGETABLES

Non-vegetarians tend to think of vegetables as side dishes—a potato and a green beside a piece of meat. Stuffed vegetables, however, are more substantial than a side dish. And they give us a more balanced meal than just vegetables would as they tend to be stuffed with grains.

CABBAGE STUFFED WITH MUSHROOMS AND BARLEY

This is a very delicate dish, despite the intensity of cabbage. All of the ingredients blend magically together to make the strong mild and the mild more assertive. Cabbage is very nutritious, so having many recipes around keeps you from growing tired of it.

1/2 cup barley	*one head of green cabbage*
1 large onion, chopped	*2 large ripe tomatoes,*
1 tablespoon olive oil	*chopped*
5 garlic cloves, chopped	*5-10 basil leaves, chopped*
1 lb. mushrooms, coarsely chopped	*1/2 teaspoon cinnamon*
2 tablespoons chopped parsley	*salt and pepper to taste*
1 tablespoon chopped dill	

Cook the barley in a pot of lightly salted water until soft, about an hour. Sauté the onions in oil until transparent. Add the garlic and stir for a minute. Remove and reserve half of the onion-garlic mixture to use for sauce. Add the mushrooms to the pan and stir until soft. Add the herbs, seasonings, and cooked barley. Simmer for a few minutes more.

Put the cabbage in a pot of boiling water and cook until the leaves get soft. Then, cut away the core of the cabbage and remove one leaf at a time, being careful not to break the leaves. Put a heaping spoonful of the barley-mushroom mix into the core side of each leaf and roll, folding in the sides. Secure with a toothpick or string.

Meanwhile, add chopped tomatoes to a pan with the reserved onion and garlic and sauté until the tomatoes are soft. Add the basil, cinnamon, and salt. Place half of the tomato sauce in the bottom of a shallow, non-stick baking pan, and place the cabbage rolls on top of the sauce. Put the remaining sauce, if any, on top of the rolls. Bake in a 350° oven for about half an hour. *Serves 4*

Nutritional analysis per serving:174 calories; 4.4 g fat (21.4% calories from fat); 0 mg cholesterol; 30.6 g carbohydrate; 6.1 g protein; 31 mg sodium; 122 mg calcium; 2.9 mg iron; 45 mg vitamin C

RED CABBAGE OR KALE STUFFED WITH RICE, RAISINS, AND WALNUTS IN ORANGE SWEET AND SOUR SAUCE

This is a far more assertive dish than the last. Red cabbage is stronger than green and kale is among the most nutritious of the leafy green vegetables. The raisins, walnuts, and sweet and sour sauce create a lovely, pungent taste, rich in beta-carotene and vitamin C.

1 bunch kale or 1 head red cabbage
1/2 cup uncooked brown rice
1/3 cup of raisins
1/3 cup chopped walnuts
1 onion, chopped
4 cloves garlic, minced
1/4 cup chopped parsley
4 tablespoons chopped dill

Steam the kale lightly, or put the cabbage in boiling water and cook until the leaves are soft. Cook the rice in 1 cup of water with the onions and garlic until almost cooked through. Add the other ingredients. Remove the heavy ribs from the kale or cabbage and put 2 tablespoons of the rice mixture at one end of the leaf. Roll and secure with a toothpick or string. Place in a non-stick baking pan with about an inch of water and bake in a 350° oven for 15 minutes. Serve with the orange sweet and sour sauce.

ORANGE SWEET AND SOUR SAUCE:
juice of 2 oranges
2 tablespoons apple cider vinegar
4 tablespoons sucanat
2 tablespoons arrowroot in 1/4 cup water

Put all the ingredients in a small saucepan and stir until lightly thickened. If gooey, add more water.
Serves 4

Nutritional analysis per serving: 280 calories; 2.9 g fat (8.9% calories from fat); 0 mg cholesterol; 60.8 g carbohydrate; 6.8 g protein; 45 mg sodium; 192 mg calcium; 4.2 mg iron; 103 mg vitamin C

STUFFED VIETNAMESE CABBAGE

This is another delicate stuffed cabbage dish with the very healthy shitake mushrooms and tree ears that are so good for the heart and fight cancer as well.

1 oz. cellophane noodles
6 dried shitake mushrooms
3 medium tree ears
6 dried lily buds
1/2 small onion or 2 shallots, minced
4 garlic cloves, minced
6 large cabbage leaves
tomato sauce (below)

Soak the noodles, mushrooms, tree ears, and lily buds in warm water until soft. Reserve the water. Coarsely chop and mix with the onions and garlic. Drop the cabbage leaves in boiling water for about a minute. Remove the hard rib at the end of each leaf. Put about 2 tablespoons of the mixture at the soft end of each leaf, fold in the sides, and roll. Make the tomato sauce.

TOMATO SAUCE:
1 small onion, minced
4 cloves garlic, minced
1 teaspoon canola oil
3 large tomatoes, chopped
2 tablespoons soy sauce or fish sauce
3 tablespoons reserved mushroom water
2 tablespoons chopped coriander

Sauté the onion and garlic in the oil in a saucepan. Add the toma-toes, soy or fish sauce, and water and cook over low heat for about 5 minutes. Put the cabbage rolls on top of the sauce and continue cooking for half an hour. Serve with rice. Sprinkle the tops with coriander.

Serves 2 to 3

Nutritional analysis per serving: 255 calories; 5.4 g fat (17.5% calories from fat); 2 mg cholesterol; 51.4 g carbohydrate; 5.4 g protein; 35 mg sodium; 93 mg calcium; 2.1 mg iron; 66 mg vitamin C

STUFFED ZUCCHINI

Zucchini is a delicious, versatile vegetable and a good source of vitamin A and calcium.

1/2 cup uncooked brown basmati rice
4 medium zucchini
1 small leek or 4 scallions, chopped
1 teaspoon olive oil
1/4 cup chopped dill
1/4 cup chopped walnuts
salt and pepper
juice of 1 lemon
1 tablespoon arrowroot

Cook the rice in 1 cup of water until al dente. Cut the zucchini in half lengthwise and scoop out the soft pulpy part, leaving about 1/4-inch around the skin of each half. Place in boiling water and cook for about 5 minutes. Remove with a slotted spoon and let cool. Sauté the leek in the olive oil and add the cooked rice, the dill, the walnuts, and salt and pepper. Stuff the zucchini with the rice mixture, place in a non-stick baking pan with the juice of a lemon and 1 inch of water, and bake in a 350° oven for 15 to 20 minutes. When the zucchini is cooked, put the liquid in a small saucepan, add about 1/2 cup water with 1 tablespoon of arrowroot dissolved in it, and stir until thickened. Pour over zucchini.

Serves 2 to 4

Nutritional analysis per serving: 154 calories; 3.2 g fat (17.6% calories from fat); 0 mg cholesterol; 29.0 g carbohydrate; 4.6 g protein; 14 mg sodium; 93 mg calcium; 2.8 mg iron; 22 mg vitamin C

SATAYS AND KABOBS

Galangal and kaffir lime leaves can be found in Thai-Vietnamese markets. Galangal is a root similar in shape to ginger with an earthier flavor. Ginger is an excellent alternative if you have no source of galangal. Ginger is one of the most medicinal of foods. It has immune-boosting and anti-inflammatory properties, and helps fight colds.

THAI TOFU SATAY

1/2 lb. tofu cut into 1-inch cubes
12 shitake mushrooms
small onions

FOR THE MARINADE:
1-inch piece galangal or ginger
2 stalks lemon grass
6 kaffir lime leaves or the zest of a lime
1 stalk coriander, with roots
5 cloves garlic
2 tablespoons soy sauce or fish sauce
1 teaspoon ground coriander seeds
1 tablespoon ground cumin
1/2 cup coconut milk (optional)

Put the solid ingredients into a spice grinder or blender and grind or blend until smooth. Put all the ingredients in a bowl and mix until smooth. Add the tofu and mushrooms and marinate for at least an hour. (It is best to leave it marinating all day.) Alternate the tofu, mushrooms, and onions on skewers. Grill or broil on all sides. Serve with peanut sauce and brown rice.

PEANUT SAUCE:
2 cloves garlic, minced
1/4 cup ground peanuts
1 tablespoon red curry paste
1/2 cup coconut milk
1 teaspoon oil (soy, safflower, sesame, or canola)
2 tablespoons fish sauce (optional)

Sauté the garlic in the oil and add the other ingredients. Stir until smooth.

Serves 4

Nutritional analysis per serving: 302 calories; 25.3 g fat (70.7% calories from fat); 2 mg cholesterol; 14.1 g carbohydrate; 9.5 g protein; 244 mg sodium; 114 mg calcium; 5.9 mg iron; 15 mg vitamin C

CHINESE TOFU KABOB

You can find uncut bamboo shoots canned in some supermarkets and all Chinese markets. You can find them fresh, soaking in water, in Chinese markets. They are like asparagus in the way they grow and have a similar short season.

1/4 cup light soy sauce
2 tablespoons rice wine
3 cloves garlic, minced
1-inch piece of ginger, minced
1 teaspoon strong sesame oil

1 tablespoon sucanat
1 lb. firm tofu or tempeh
8 shitake mushrooms
1 large bamboo shoot
8 shallots or small
white onions

Place the soy sauce, rice wine, garlic, ginger, sesame oil, and sucanat in a baking dish or other dish large enough to held the tofu or tempeh. Stir all the ingredients together and put the tofu or tempeh (or both) on top. If the tofu is very thick, cut it in half first. Marinate it for a day, if possible, or for an hour at least. Turn at least once. Soak the mushrooms in water until soft. Cut the bamboo shoot into 1-inch pieces and the tofu/tempeh into 1-inch cubes. Peel the shallots or onions, but leave them whole. Put the tofu, mushrooms, and bamboo shoots on a skewer with onions or shallots at the ends. Cook on a gas grill or under a broiler for about 8 minutes per side. As only the onions are truly raw, the cooking time is less critical than with some dishes unless you use fresh bamboo shoots.

Serves 4

Nutritional analysis per serving: 187 calories; 6.7 g fat (31.5% calories from fat); 0 mg cholesterol; 20.7 g carbohydrate; 12.4 g protein; 1052 mg sodium; 145 mg calcium; 7.2 mg iron; 5 mg vitamin C

MIDDLE EASTERN KABOBS

Seitan, which is made from wheat gluten, and tofu, which is bean curd, are not traditional Middle Eastern fare, but they work well as alternatives to meat. I've chosen seitan here because it is meatier than tofu. You might forget all meat substitutes and just use vegetables.

3 cloves garlic, minced	*1 medium zucchini*
1 small onion, minced	*1 Japanese or other small eggplant*
2 tablespoons cumin	*1 green pepper*
juice of a lemon	*8 large cherry tomatoes*
1 lb. tofu or seitan	*8 small white onions*

Put the garlic, onion, cumin, and lemon juice in a dish large enough to hold the tofu or seitan and the eggplant and zucchini. Cut the tofu or seitan into approximately 1-inch squares and slice the eggplant and zucchini into rounds. Steam the eggplant and zucchini for about 3 minutes as they will require more cooking than the other ingredients. Cut the pepper in half lengthwise, remove the stem and seeds, then cut it into 1- to 2-inch squares. Put the tofu or seitan and the eggplant and zucchini into the marinade, marinating for at least an hour—for the day, if possible. Turn at least once. Put all of the ingredients on skewers with the onions at the ends to hold everything on. Grill as in the recipe for Chinese tofu kabob, but for a few minutes more as the vegetables need more cooking.

Serves 4

Nutritional analysis per serving: 338 calories; 7.8 g fat (18.8% calories from fat); 0 mg cholesterol; 58.2 g carbohydrate; 17.3 g protein; 58 mg sodium; 327 mg calcium; 10.6 mg iron; 106 mg vitamin C

INDIAN KABOBS

A kabob (which means minced) is traditionally made from lamb, chicken, or fish. However, I have found a non-meat recipe in *Classic Indian Vegetarian and Grain Cooking* by Julie Sahni. In her recipe, the kabob is deep-fried and cooked more like a burger. In the recipe I have adapted, the kabob is grilled.

1 cup yellow split peas
2-1/2 cups water
1 large yellow onion, chopped
3 cloves garlic, minced
1/4-inch piece ginger, minced
1/2 teaspoon ground cardamom
1 teaspoon ground cumin
1/4 teaspoon cayenne
1/2 cup chopped mushrooms
1 teaspoon canola oil
1/4 cup fresh coriander
2 green chilis (optional)
1 tablespoon lemon juice
1 cup whole wheat bread crumbs
8 small onions
8 cremini (or other firm mushrooms)
1 green pepper, cut into 1-inch squares

Soak the split peas in water for at least 4 hours. Drain and bring to a boil in a pot with 2-1/2 cups water, 1/4 cup of the chopped onions (reserving the rest for later), the garlic, ginger, cardamom, cumin, and cayenne. Cook over medium heat for about 30 minutes, or until the peas are cooked but not mushy and the water is absorbed. If there is still water, cook over high heat until it has evaporated.

While the peas are cooking, sauté the rest of the onion in oil until yellow, then add the mushrooms and cook until soft, about 3 minutes. Purée the onions, mushrooms, and coriander (and chilis, if a hotter kabob is desired) in a food processor and add the cooked split peas. The mixture should be well blended, but with a little texture. Put the mixture in a bowl and add bread crumbs and lemon juice. Work it with the hands until it attains the consistency of a soft dough, then form into oblong balls, about 2 inches long. Place them in the top of a steamer and steam for about 5 minutes. Allow to cool, remove from the steamer and place on skewers, alternating with the onions, mushrooms, and peppers. Then cook on a gas grill or under a broiler, turning every few minutes, until browned on all sides. Serve with brown rice.

Serves 4

Nutritional analysis per serving: 448 calories; 4.4 g fat (8.5% calories from fat); 0 mg cholesterol; 85.6 g carbohydrate; 21.7 g protein; 245 mg sodium; 217 mg calcium; 5.9 mg iron; 61 mg vitamin C

STIR-FRIES

PAD THAI

Most of the work for this dish involves the chopping and preparing of foods before cooking. Pad Thai cooks very quickly.

1 teaspoon canola oil
3 cloves garlic, minced
2 tablespoons egg substitute, mixed with 2-3 tablespoons water (found in health food stores)
1/2 lb. rice noodles (1/8-inch wide)*
juice of a lemon
2-3 tablespoons soy sauce or fish sauce*
1/2 teaspoon sucanat
2 tablespoons chopped roasted peanuts
1 tablespoon chopped preserved turnip or radish*
1/2 lb. bean sprouts
1/4 teaspoon chili powder
4 tablespoons chopped coriander leaves
2 scallions, sliced
1/2 lb. tofu, cut in 1-inch cubes
1/4 lb. snow peas, lightly steamed

Soak the noodles in water until soft. If rice noodles aren't available, use Udon noodles, cooked until al dente. Sauté the garlic lightly in the oil in a wok or large pan and add egg substitute. Stir quickly and add the drained noodles. Stir until coated. Add all the other ingredients, keeping some coriander, tofu, and snow peas to place on top. You can substitute broccoli for the snow peas or use both.

Serves 4

Nutritional analysis per serving: 368 calories; 8.4 g fat (20.0% calories from fat); 2 mg cholesterol; 66.9 g carbohydrate; 9.0 g protein; 89 mg sodium; 112 mg calcium; 5.8 mg iron; 35 mg vitamin C

(*found in Thai and other Asian markets)

❀ ❀

SOBA NOODLES WITH VEGETABLES

Japanese soba noodles are made with buckwheat, which isn't wheat at all, so they are particularly good for people who love pasta but have an intolerance for wheat. With the broccoli, ginger, garlic, and shitake mushrooms, this is another wonderful anticancer dish. You could add 1/4 pound of cubed tofu as a variation.

1/2 lb. soba noodles
1/4 lb. snow peas
about 12 shitake mushrooms
1 cup broccoli flowers
1 teaspoon light sesame oil
2 tablespoons soy sauce
1 teaspoon grated ginger
3 cloves minced garlic
1 teaspoon sucanat
2 scallions, sliced, white and 1/2 green
2 tablespoons mirin

Soak shitake mushrooms in water (if using dried). Steam the broccoli for about 4 minutes. Add the snow peas and steam another minute. Cook the soba noodles in a pot of boiling water until tender, about 8 minutes. Heat the oil in a pan and sauté the garlic lightly. Add the ginger and scallions and sauté about 1 minute. Add the steamed vegetables, soy sauce, mirin, and sucanat, and stir together. Put the noodles in a bowl and add vegetable mixture. Mix together and serve.

Serves 2

Nutritional analysis per serving: 572 calories; 3.9 g fat (5.8% calories from fat); 0 mg cholesterol; 118.2 g carbohydrate; 25.3 g protein; 2087 mg sodium; 137 mg calcium; 6.1 mg iron; 110 mg vitamin C

VEGETABLES WITH RED CURRY SAUCE

While a Thai cookbook might provide many recipes with various combinations of vegetables and sauces, I have chosen the most popular sauce to use with any variety of vegetables. I provide you with a list of possible vegetables, and you can choose two or more for any dish. Some Thai curries are made with coconut milk, but many health conscious people don't like to use coconut as it contains saturated fats. The dishes are delicious either way. The coconut milk makes a richer sauce, and if you eat no meat, can be used occasionally without fear of overloading on saturated fats. An alternative would be to add some dried coconut to fat-free soy milk.

RED CURRY SAUCE:
4 dried red chilis
2 tablespoons coriander seed
1 tablespoon cumin seed
2 stalks lemongrass, white only*
4 kaffir lime leaves* or zest of 1/2 lime
1-inch piece galangal* or ginger
1 shallot

Place all the ingredients in a spice grinder or processor and grind to a paste.

THE VEGETABLES:
Broccoli, zucchini, snap peas or snow peas, stringbeans or long beans, carrots (sliced), baby corn, cauliflower, bok choy, eggplant (cubed), water chestnuts, bamboo shoots, tree ears, shitake, straw or white mushrooms

continued

(* found in Thai and other Asian markets)

1 teaspoon vegetable oil
3 garlic cloves, chopped
2 tablespoons soy sauce or fish sauce*
1/2 teaspoon sucanat
1-inch piece galangal or ginger, chopped
1 stalk lemon grass, sliced
2 tablespoons red curry paste
about 10 basil leaves (Thai basil is somewhat milder than ours)
1 cup unsweetened coconut milk (optional)

If using tree ears or shitake mushrooms, soak them in water until soft. Sauté the garlic in oil in a wok or pan for a few seconds and add red curry paste. Stir about 10 seconds, then add 2 tablespoons of water, soy sauce or fish sauce, and galangal. Stir and add the vegetables. Cook over low heat until al dente. It is possible to steam the vegetables lightly first and then stir-fry them in the wok at the last minute. (Snow peas and snap peas can be left till the last minute.) Add the basil and (optional) coconut milk and mix all the ingredients together. Remove from heat and serve.

Serves 4 to 6

Nutritional analysis per serving: 189 calories; 13.3 g fat (57.3% calories from fat); 1 mg cholesterol; 17.5 g carbohydrate; 4.8 g protein; 36 mg sodium; 92 mg calcium; 4.2 mg iron; 126 mg vitamin C

(*can be found in some health food stores and in Thai and other Asian markets)

TOFU WITH MUSHROOMS AND BROCCOLI

This particular combination, simply prepared without a curry, is so delicate and fragrant that I include it separately.

1/4 cup vegetable stock
1 tablespoon arrowroot
3 cloves garlic, minced
1/2 lb. white mushrooms
2 broccoli stems, sliced lengthwise, 1/2-inch thick
1 carrot, finely sliced
2 tablespoons soy sauce or fish sauce
1/2 teaspoon sucanat
1/2 lb. firm tofu

Dissolve the arrowroot in stock, reserving 2 tablespoons for the garlic. Steam the broccoli, carrots, and mushrooms about 3 minutes. Heat the reserved stock in a wok or pan and sauté the garlic for a few seconds. Add the tofu, soy sauce or fish sauce, and sugar and stir to coat the tofu. Add the broccoli, carrots, and mushrooms and stir another minute. Pour in the stock and stir until thickened. This dish can be made with broccoli stems or stems with flowers. It is a great dish for using stems that might otherwise be wasted.

Serves 2

Nutritional analysis per serving: 263 calories; 9.2 g fat (28.4% calories from fat); 3 mg cholesterol; 34.4 g carbohydrate; 17.9 g protein; 277 mg sodium; 229 mg calcium; 9.5 mg iron; 171 mg vitamin C

POTATO CURRY

This is another Thai curry that can be used along with a mixed or single vegetable curry.

3 potatoes, cut in 1-inch cubes
3 cloves garlic, minced
1 stalk lemongrass
1 teaspoon ground coriander
1 tablespoon minced galangal or ginger
1 teaspoon canola oil
2 tablespoons soy sauce or fish sauce
1/2 teaspoon sucanat
1 tablespoon curry powder
1 cup coconut milk
1/2 cup vegetable stock
4 shallots, halved

Grind the lemongrass, galangal, garlic, and coriander in a food processor. Heat the oil in a wok or pan and add the paste. Stir and add the coconut milk. When well-combined, add the potatoes. Then, mix in the soy sauce or fish sauce, sugar, curry powder, and vegetable stock. Stir together well and add shallot halves. Simmer until the potatoes are cooked.

Serves 2

Nutritional analysis per serving: 744 calories; 35.0 g fat (40.4% calories from fat); 3 mg cholesterol; 101.6 g carbohydrate; 14.5 g protein; 464 mg sodium; 96 mg calcium; 7.1 mg iron; 93 mg vitamin C

ORANGE-FLAVORED SEITAN

Seitan is a good source of protein and an excellent meat substitute. This recipe is rich in beta-carotene and vitamin C.

1/2 lb. seitan
2 tablespoons soy sauce
juice of 1/2 orange
2 teaspoons rice wine (optional)
1 tablespoon minced ginger
1 teaspoon arrowroot
2 tablespoons canola oil
2 cloves garlic, minced
zest of an orange, in 1-inch pieces
2 dried chilis, sliced lengthwise
1 red pepper cut in 2-inch pieces
about 1/4 cup snow peas or broccoli

Slice the seitan as thin as possible and mix it in a bowl with the soy sauce, orange juice, rice wine, ginger, sesame oil, and arrowroot. Marinate for about 1/2 hour. Remove the seitan from the marinade with a slotted spoon, and reserve the marinade. Heat the oil in a wok until it is very hot. Add the seitan and stir-fry for a few minutes until the seitan darkens and is crisp. Reduce the heat and add the garlic, stirring for a few seconds. Then add the chilis, orange peel, and peppers, stirring briefly. Add the marinade and cover for a few minutes to cook the red pepper (or steam the pepper in advance). If too dry, add a bit more soy sauce and a couple of tablespoons of water or stock. Add the snow peas or broccoli and stir for another minute or two until the peas are cooked and the sauce thickened.

Serves 2

Nutritional analysis per serving: 260 calories; 21.0 g fat (21.3% calories from fat); 0 mg cholesterol; 13.5 g carbohydrate; 160.9 g protein; 1648 mg sodium; 46 mg calcium; 1.4 mg iron; 149 mg vitamin C

STIR-FRIED SEITAN WITH VEGETABLES

This is a basic Chinese stir-fry that uses seitan, which is a good source of protein and an excellent meat substitute.

1 small onion, roasted
3 cloves garlic, minced
1 teaspoon minced ginger
1/4 cup broth
1/2 lb. seitan
6 shitake mushrooms soaked in water (save the water)
1 cup shredded napa cabbage or sliced bok choy
1/4 lb. spinach, cleaned and shredded
2 tablespoons light soy sauce
2 tablespoons rice wine
1/4 teaspoon five-spices powder (optional)
1 teaspoon arrowroot

Slice the onion and in a non-stick pan or wok, sauté with the garlic, ginger, and 1 tablespoon of the stock until the garlic is soft (about 1 minute). Add the seitan, mushrooms, and five-spices powder, stirring until they are coated with the onion, garlic, and ginger mixture. Add the cabbage, spinach, and all of the liquid except the mushroom water and cook until the cabbage and spinach are soft. Add the arrowroot to about 2 tablespoons of mushroom water and stir until dissolved. Pour into the pan or wok and stir until the sauce is lightly thickened.

Serves 2

Nutritional analysis per serving: 197 calories; 8.0 g fat (8.8% calories from fat); 0 mg cholesterol; 23.7 g carbohydrate; 162.1 g protein; 877 mg sodium; 122 mg calcium; 2.2 mg iron; 41 mg vitamin C

COMFORT FOODS

BAKED POLENTA WITH ZUCCHINI
AND TOMATO SAUCE

This recipe turns a simple grain into a gourmet meal. Polenta is solid but pliant, almost like a dumpling in texture.

1 red pepper	1/2 cup basil, lightly chopped
1 cup polenta (cornmeal)	1 medium leek, sliced
3 cups water	2 small zucchini, sliced
1 cup tomato sauce (see page 121)	1/2 lb. mushrooms, sliced
1/2 cup soy parmesan	1 teaspoon olive oil

Roast a red pepper under the broiler. While it is cooking, boil the water in a heavy pot. Keep turning the pepper on all sides until it is lightly charred. Slowly add the polenta to the water, stirring with a wooden spoon until the polenta comes away from the sides of the pan (15 to 20 minutes). Turn it out onto a wooden board, smooth to about 1/2-inch thick, and let it cool.

Meanwhile, make the tomato sauce and put it in the bottom of a baking pan. Slice the polenta into 2-inch squares or triangles and place it on top of the tomato sauce. Sprinkle the top with the soy parmesan and half the basil. When the pepper is cooked and cool enough to touch, peel it and cut it into 1-inch pieces, removing the ribs and the seeds. Place the pepper pieces amongst the polenta pieces. Sauté the leeks, zucchini, and mushrooms (adding in that order) in oil until lightly brown but not too soft. Put them on top of the polenta. Bake in a 350° oven for about 15 minutes until bubbly. Sprinkle with the rest of the basil, cook for another few minutes, and serve.

Serves 4

Nutritional analysis per serving: 220 calories; 4.2 g fat (16.0% calories from fat); 0 mg cholesterol; 38.5 g carbohydrate; 11.6 g protein; 644 mg sodium; 1477 mg calcium; 3.0 mg iron; 49 mg vitamin C

ITALIAN GRILLED VEGETABLES
WITH POLENTA

One of the real downsides of eating healthy food is giving up charcoal grilling. Charcoal is carcinogenic and should be avoided, except for pure wood charcoals. There is some evidence that any quick cooking that burns food is carcinogenic, so I would restrict all grilling on a regular basis. But an occasional grilling, carefully done, should not be ruled out. I recommend a gas grill. This dish is wonderful with or without the polenta, and the vegetables can be varied.

1 eggplant	2 large portebello mushrooms
2 zucchini	2 large endive or radicchio
2 tomatoes	1 tablespoon chopped garlic
2 red onions	1 tablespoon olive oil
1 fennel bulb	a sprig or two each of basil,
2 red peppers	oregano, rosemary
juice of 1 lemon	

Cut the eggplant lengthwise into slices about 1/4- to 1/2-inch wide. Sprinkle with salt and let sit for at least 15 minutes until it sweats, then dry with paper towels (this gets rid of the bitterness). Mince the garlic and mix in olive oil, then divide into three portions. Add one minced herb to each portion and brush each vegetable, except the peppers, with one infusion. Add salt and pepper, if desired.

Cut the zucchini in half lengthwise and marinate it in the oregano infusion and some lemon juice. (If the zucchini is large, cut it into 1/4-inch slices.) Cut the tomatoes in half and marinate them in the basil infusion. Cut the onions in half and cover them with the oregano infusion. Cut the fennel into four pieces and the endive in half. Drizzle them with lemon juice and salt. Marinate the portebello mushrooms in the rosemary infusion.

When the eggplant is dry, marinate it in any one, or a mix of the herb infusions. Leave the peppers whole while grilling, turning them

continued

when they start to char (at least four times). When the peppers are cooked, remove the skin and cut them in half lengthwise, removing the seeds and membranes. Grill the vegetables on a gas or electric grill until lightly browned and grill marks appear (a stovetop grill is a good alternative). Then turn and cook on the other side, brushing with the infusions. Meanwhile, cook the polenta.

POLENTA:
1-1/2 cups cornmeal (for checkerboard polenta, 3/4 cup
yellow, 3/4 cup blue)
6 cups water
1/2 cup soy parmesan
1 teaspoon salt

Boil the water in saucepan, then add the salt and polenta. Stir frequently until the polenta is smooth (about 20 minutes unless you're using instant polenta). Add the soy parmesan. Spread onto a plate or pan and let cool. Cut into 2-inch squares and arrange in checkerboard pattern. Bake about 10 minutes. Serve by placing a checkerboard of polenta on each plate and arranging the vegetables around it.

Serves 4

Nutritional analysis per serving: 270 calories; 2.5 g fat (7.6% calories from fat); 0 mg cholesterol; 59.0 g carbohydrate; 10.1 g protein; 97 mg sodium; 209 mg calcium; 5.4 mg iron; 125 mg vitamin C

JAPANESE GRILLED VEGETABLES WITH TOFU

This version of grilled vegetables, together with tofu, makes a complete meal. It can be served with brown rice, which, with the tofu, makes a complete protein.

2 Japanese eggplants
2 zucchini
8 shitake mushrooms
1 lb. firm tofu
2 leeks
1 teaspoon miso in 1/4 cup water
pinch of chili powder (optional)

1/4 cup soy sauce
2 tablespoons ginger
1 teaspoon sesame oil
3-4 cloves garlic, minced
1 tablespoon sucanat (optional)

Mix all the ingredients on the right in a bowl to make the marinade. Drain the tofu, cut into 1-inch slices, and marinate for at least an hour. You can marinate the vegetables in the same marinade or make a separate one for them. Grill on a gas, electric, or stovetop grill until browned on both sides.

Serves 2

Nutritional analysis per serving: 408 calories; 14.4 g fat (28.5% calories from fat); 0 mg cholesterol; 53.5 g carbohydrate; 27.5 g protein; 2197 mg sodium; 303 mg calcium; 14.8 mg iron; 20 mg vitamin C

SWEET POTATO RING WITH
BRUSSELS SPROUTS

This zesty dish, with cranberries, is an excellent addition to the
Thanksgiving meal.

FOR THE RING:
4 large sweet potatoes or yams
zest of 2 oranges, using zester, or mincing skins
2 tablespoons maple syrup (optional)
1/2 cup soy milk

Boil the sweet potatoes until soft, then peel and mash, using a food
mill, ricer, potato masher, or food processor. Put in a bowl and add
the orange zest, maple syrup, and soy milk. Mix until smooth. Put
the mixture in a lightly oiled ring mold and bake in a 350° oven for
about 15 minutes. Meanwhile, prepare brussels sprouts:

1/4 cup slivered almonds or chopped walnuts
1 teaspoon olive oil
1 lb. brussels sprouts
2 tablespoons chopped dill

Steam the brussels sprouts until tender. Sauté the nuts in olive oil
until slightly brown. Mix the nuts and dill with the brussels
sprouts. Unmold the yams and put the brussels sprouts into the
center of the ring.

Serves 6 to 8

Nutritional analysis per serving: 231 calories; 4.1 g fat (15.2% calories from
fat); 0 mg cholesterol; 46.1 g carbohydrate; 5.8 g protein; 36 mg sodium; 96
mg calcium; 2.3 mg iron; 71 mg vitamin C

POTATO CROQUETTES

In Indian cuisine, there are many kinds of pakoras. Unfortunately these wonderful vegetable savories are coated with batter and deep-fried. As deep-frying is not an acceptable method of cooking, I have mixed the batter ingredients with the potatoes and broiled them. The results are delicious.

4 potatoes, boiled until soft
1/2 teaspoon turmeric
1/2 teaspoon garam masala
*   or curry powder*
1 teaspoon canola oil
1/2 teaspoon mustard seeds
1 onion, chopped
3 cloves garlic, chopped

1-2 chilis, chopped
1 cup chickpea flour
1 cup warm water
1/2 teaspoon baking powder
salt to taste
4 tablespoons fresh coriander,
chopped

Peel and mash the potatoes and add the turmeric and curry powder or garam masala. Heat the oil in a pan and add the mustard seeds. Cover until they stop spattering. Then add the onion, garlic, and chilis and cook until soft. Add this to the potatoes.

Mix the chickpea flour, baking powder, and salt in a separate bowl. Add the water slowly and mix until it reaches a consistency that is neither thick nor watery. Add this to the potatoes with the coriander and mix together until smooth. Form into patties the shape of hamburgers and broil until they turn light brown. Serve with mango chutney.

Serves 2 to 4

Nutritional analysis per serving: 1001 calories; 7.4g fat (6.4% calories from fat); 0 mg cholesterol; 216.5 g carbohydrate; 26.5 g protein; 258 mg sodium; 338 mg calcium; 11.4 mg iron; 304 mg vitamin C

POTATO "LASAGNE"

The lowly potato can be turned into an elegant base for a wonderful, lasagne-like dish. It requires slicing the potatoes paper thin. I use a mandoline, a hand-held slicer, which makes thinner slices than my food processor and doesn't require that I cut them in half to fit them in. You could make this with any number of fillings. Serve these thinly sliced potatoes lightly sautéed in olive oil as an entrée or side dish.

3 large potatoes
1 small onion, chopped
5 cloves garlic, minced
1 tablespoon olive oil
1/2 lb. mushrooms
2 medium tomatoes
1/4 cup chopped basil

1/4 cup chopped parsley
1/4 lb. soy mozzarella
or firm tofu
3 tablespoons soy parmesan
1/2 lb. spinach
1 small leek

Slice the potatoes paper-thin lengthwise. Use a non-stick baking dish or brush with olive oil. Put a layer of overlapping slices of potatoes on the bottom of the baking dish. It should look like fish scales or flower petals. Sauté the onions and garlic in the olive oil until transparent. Add the mushrooms and cook for another two minutes. Spread this on top of the potatoes, then cover with a layer of sliced tomatoes and a sprinkling of the herbs. Add another layer of the potatoes. On top of that, put well-washed and lightly chopped spinach leaves, thinly sliced leeks, chopped soy mozzarella or crumbled tofu, the rest of the herbs, and the soy parmesan. Cover with another layer of potatoes. Bake in a 350° oven until browned on top and bubbly, about 20 minutes.

Serves 4

Nutritional analysis per serving: 1330 calories; 253.8 g fat (46.5% calories from fat); 0 mg cholesterol; 340.2 g carbohydrate; 316.3g protein; 1239 mg sodium; 3539 mg calcium; 13.4 mg iron; 299 mg vitamin C

FALAFEL

The falafel from Middle Eastern markets is delicious, but virtually everything in it is fried. The good news is you can make it without frying anything. Use a falafel mix or make it yourself following the recipe below.

1/2 cup chickpeas
1/2 cup yellow split peas
1 small onion, chopped
2 cloves garlic, minced
1 tablespoon cumin
2 tablespoons chopped parsley

Soak the beans and peas in about 3 cups of water for a day. Drain and put all the ingredients into a food processor. Blend well until they form a damp paste. It shouldn't be sticky, but should hold together easily. You can add water if it is too dry, but add it slowly to get the right consistency. Form into small patties, about 1 inch in diameter. Now you can either steam them or cook them like dumplings, in a pot of boiling water.

Meanwhile, prepare the accompaniments:

1 small eggplant, cut into rounds and sprinkled with salt
1 medium potato, cut into rounds
1 cucumber, sliced
2 small tomatoes, sliced
6 pita breads
shredded lettuce
*   (romaine, crisp green leaf, or other crisp lettuce)*
1 cup tahini sauce (see below)

continued

Sprinkle the eggplant with salt and let it sweat for about 15 minutes, then wipe it dry with a paper towel. Put the steamed or boiled falafel, the eggplant, and the potatoes under the broiler until light brown. Turn and broil on the other side. Put two pieces of falafel, a slice or two of eggplant, a few slices of potato, cucumber, and tomato into a pita bread. Top with the shredded lettuce and tahini sauce and serve.

TAHINI SAUCE:
1/2 cup tahini
juice of 1 lemon
2 garlic cloves, minced
parsley, dill, or coriander, minced
1/2-1 cup water

Mix all the ingredients together, slowly adding the water until the sauce is pourable but not watery.
Serves 4 to 6

Nutritional analysis per serving: 380 calories; 3.5 g fat (7.9% calories from fat); 0 mg cholesterol; 75.9 g carbohydrate; 16.9 g protein; 362 mg sodium; 80 mg calcium; 5.5 mg iron; 31 mg vitamin C

VEGETABLES AS SIDE DISHES

STIR-FRIED SWEET POTATOES

Well, you are going to use sweet potatoes and not yams, although they may be called yams in your market. Sweet potatoes are resplendent with vitamin A and carotenes, while yams just aren't.

2 sweet potatoes, cut julienne and steamed
1-inch piece ginger, minced
2 tablespoons rice wine
2 tablespoons soy sauce
1 teaspoon sesame seeds
1 teaspoon light sesame oil

Sauté the ginger in the oil and add the julienned, steamed sweet potatoes. Stir for a minute and add other ingredients.

Serves 2 to 4

Nutritional analysis per serving: 205 calories; 3.2 g fat (14.8% calories from fat); 0 mg cholesterol; 38.8 g carbohydrate; 3.2 g protein; 698 mg sodium; 54 mg calcium; 1.4 mg iron; 22 mg vitamin C

SPICY EGGPLANT

This dish, despite its brash ingredients, is actually quite delicate. Cook it gently.

2-4 small eggplants
2 tablespoons soy sauce or fish sauce
1 teaspoon sucanat
1 tablespoon rice vinegar
2-3 dried chilis, crushed with seeds removed
  (or 1 red fresh chili)
6 cloves garlic, minced
4 scallions, chopped
1-inch piece ginger, minced
1 teaspoon canola oil
2 tablespoons hoisin sauce
2 tablespoons chopped basil or coriander for garnish

Eggplants soak up oil like sponges. How do you get them soft and flavorful without resorting to the use of oil? The best way is to char them on top of a gas burner (electric will do, and a broiler is a third choice). Charring small eggplants takes just a few minutes. Put the eggplant right on top of the burner with a fairly high flame and turn it on all sides. It will char quickly and usually cooks through fairly well. Once it is charred, remove it to a plate and let it cool enough to touch it. Then remove the charred skin. Cut the eggplants lengthwise in 4 to 8 pieces, depending on their size.

Next, sauté the onions, garlic, and ginger in the oil in a wok or skillet. When soft, add the eggplants and all the other ingredients and stir-fry for about 5 minutes. If they get too dry, you can add a few tablespoons of water or broth.

continued

Usually, I prefer cooking vegetables quickly. This dish, however, gains from long, slow, simmering.

Serve topped with a sprinkle of chopped coriander or basil with rice.

Serves 4

Nutritional analysis per serving: 143 calories; 3.9 g fat (22.7% calories from fat); 2 mg cholesterol; 25.9 g carbohydrate; 3.6 g protein; 14 mg sodium; 43 mg calcium; 1.5 mg iron; 144 mg vitamin C

SAUTÉED RED CABBAGE

This is another way to use cabbage, which is on the top ten list of health-giving foods. You can find meatless (usually soy) bacon substitutes in health food stores. Smoked tofu is another possible substitute.

1 small head red cabbage, shredded
1 medium onion, thinly sliced
4 cloves garlic, chopped
1/4 cup bacon substitute
1 cup broth
1 tablespoon olive oil

Sauté the onion slowly in the olive oil until golden brown. Add the garlic and stir another minute. Add the shredded cabbage, stir to coat, and add broth and bacon substitute. Cook slowly until soft and tender (about 15 minutes).

Serves 2 to 4

Nutritional analysis per serving: 235 calories; 6.5 g fat (16.9% calories from fat); 1 mg cholesterol; 55.1 g carbohydrate; 16.9 g protein; 946 mg sodium; 151 mg calcium; 2.0 mg iron; 144 mg vitamin C

RUTABAGA PURÉE WITH ROASTED GARLIC

This dish is simple and surprisingly delicious. Rutabaga is a yellow turnip, much richer in flavor and also in carotenes.

> 3 *medium rutabagas*
> 1 *large head garlic*
> 1 *teaspoon olive oil*
> 2 *sprigs fresh thyme*
> *sea salt*

Peel the rutabagas, cut into quarters, and boil (or steam) in enough water to cover until soft. Put the garlic in a roasting pan and sprinkle with olive oil and thyme leaves. Roast, unpeeled, in a 400° oven until soft but not burned. When cooked, cool and squeeze garlic out of their skins. Purée the rutabagas and the garlic together with a taste of salt. Serve with thyme sprinkled on top.

> *Serves 2 to 4*

Nutritional analysis per serving: 69 calories; 1.6 g fat (18.8% calories from fat); 0 mg cholesterol; 13.3 g carbohydrate; 2.0 g protein; 30 mg sodium; 110 mg calcium; 3.4 mg iron; 36 mg vitamin C

BROCCOLI PURÉE

This recipe is delicious and will fool anyone who dislikes broccoli. Why bother? Because it is rich in antioxidants and phytochemicals and is a must for a cancer-fighting diet.

1 head broccoli
1 small onion, minced
3 cloves garlic, minced
1/2 lb. tofu
1 small bunch of basil, tarragon, or dill
1/2 cup fat-free soy milk
1 tablespoon miso (optional)
2 tablespoons casein-free soy parmesan

Remove the flowers from the broccoli and break into florets. Peel the stems carefully, cut into thick slices, and steam for about 10 minutes. Then add the flowers and steam for another 5 minutes. Sauté the onions and garlic in a non-stick pan until soft (or use just a drop of olive oil) and add the tofu. Stir for a minute or two. Put all the ingredients in a food processor and process until smooth. If too thick, add a bit more soy milk.

Serves 2 to 4

Nutritional analysis per serving: 494 calories; 15.4 g fat (24.9% calories from fat); 0 mg cholesterol; 60.2 g carbohydrate; 44.3 g protein; 1027 mg sodium; 2038 mg calcium; 18.0 mg iron; 445 mg vitamin C

STIR-FRIED BROCCOLI

Nothing could be simpler than this dish, and very little could be better for you. Broccoli is a cruciferous vegetable and is rich in cancer-fighting substances as well as antioxidant vitamins A and C. It is also a good source of fiber. Garlic helps boost the immune system, reduces cholesterol, fights cancer, and more. Ginger has antibacterial and antifungal properties and is good for the digestive system. Add a handful of shitake mushrooms, which are anticancer and antiviral, and this delicious meal will fight whatever ails you.

1 head broccoli
5 cloves garlic, chopped
1-inch piece ginger, slivered
4-5 shitake mushrooms, soaked and sliced (optional)
1 teaspoon light sesame oil
2 tablespoons light soy sauce
3 tablespoons stock

Remove the stems from the broccoli, peel, cut into 1/2-inch slices, and steam for about 5 minutes. Cut the rest of the broccoli into florets. Sauté the garlic and ginger in oil until soft and add the broccoli stems and florets, the optional shitake mushrooms, and the stock and soy sauce. Stir-fry over low heat for a few minutes until the florets are lightly cooked. Serve with brown rice.

Serves 2 to 4

Nutritional analysis per serving: 80 calories; 2.3 g fat (22.40% calories from fat); 0 mg cholesterol; 12.3 g carbohydrate; 5.8 g protein; 831 mg sodium; 85 mg calcium; 1.8 mg iron; 143 mg vitamin C

DESSERTS

Most cakes, cookies, and custards are made with butter, sugar, and eggs. Consequently desserts are the hardest part of the meal to prepare without dairy, fat, and a debilitating amount of sugar. Even though sucanat, honey, maple syrup, barley, and rice syrups are far less harmful than bleached white sugar, they are still sugars. Most of these desserts require a minimum of sweetener.

FRUIT TART

The single hardest thing to make healthy is dessert, and pastry crust is the most difficult. I've tried substitute recipes that call for a drop of oil and water and they taste like cardboard. I've seen recipes that substitute nuts for oil, and while nuts have far more nutrients than oils, they are still fatty. I have used a soy margarine with good results, but I generally stay away from margarine. The one I chose was low in saturated fats and contained no chemicals and additives. Choose carefully and read labels. Canola oil may be the best option, but you must place it in the freezer for about an hour beforehand to work.

> 2 cups whole wheat pastry flour, or a mix of whole wheat
>   and unbleached white flours
> 1/4 cup canola oil
> 1/2 cup cold water

It is best if all of the ingredients are very cold. Put them in the freezer for about an hour. If you want a slightly lighter dough, use some unbleached white flour. Put the flour in a bowl and add the oil. Mix until blended and slowly add water, mixing with your hands as you do, until the dough is soft and pliant, but not mushy. Knead it for a few minutes to make it smooth. Divide the dough into two balls. Sprinkle surface with some flour and roll out the dough to about 1/16 of an inch.

> CUSTARD:
> 1/2 cup cold soy milk
> 2 tablespoons arrowroot
> 4 tablespoons maple syrup

Put the arrowroot and the cold soy milk in a saucepan and dissolve. Warm slowly and stir with a wire whisk until thickened, but not too thick. Add the maple syrup and stir.

Next, put the pastry crust in a lightly oiled non-stick pie tin and cover the crust with beans to hold it down while baking. Bake in a 350° oven until crisp and golden (10 to 15 minutes).

Remove the crust from the oven and fill it with the custard. Top with one or more of the following fruits: raspberries, blackberries, blueberries, strawberries, sliced kiwi. Then, warm sugarless raspberry jam to a thick liquid in a saucepan and glaze the tart.

ROLLED OAT PASTRY

This pastry crust is low in fat.

1 cup whole wheat pastry flour
1 cup rolled oats
1/2 cup ground walnuts, pecans, hazelnuts, or almonds
2 tablespoons canola oil
1/4 cup maple syrup
1/4 cup water
1/2 teaspoon cinnamon

Sift the flour into a bowl and add the rolled oats, cinnamon, and nuts. Whisk the maple syrup and oil together and add to the dry ingredients. Slowly add the water until a pliable consistency is reached. Rub oil on a 9-inch pie tin, or use a non-stick pan. This is not a pastry you can roll out—it will fall apart. Instead, put the dough into the tin and spread it with your fingers until it covers evenly, about 1/8-inch thick.

Nutritional analysis per serving: 146 calories; 4.3 g fat (25.8% calories from fat); 0 mg cholesterol; 24.4 g carbohydrate; 3.7 g protein; 2 mg sodium; 22 mg calcium; 1.2 mg iron; 0 mg vitamin C

APPLE PIE

This may not be mom's apple pie, but everything in it is good for you and it is not a sacrifice.

1 recipe pastry crust or rolled oat pastry
4 apples, cored, peeled, and sliced
1 teaspoon cinnamon
1/4 cup apple juice
2 tablespoons arrowroot
2 tablespoons maple syrup

Make a crust as above and put it into a non-stick pie tin. Place the apple slices in the dough and sprinkle with cinnamon. Dissolve the arrowroot in cold apple juice in a small saucepan and warm over low heat, stirring until thickened. Add the maple syrup and stir for another minute. Pour over the apples. Put another layer of crust on top, pressing edges together. Bake in a 350° oven for 20 minutes.

Nutritional analysis per serving: 198 calories; 4.6 g fat (20.0% calories from fat); 0 mg cholesterol; 37.9 g carbohydrate; 3.9 g protein; 3 mg sodium; 45 mg calcium; 1.9 mg iron; 4 mg vitamin C

APPLE CRUNCH

This is a very delicious way of making a low-fat dessert. Everything in it is nutritious.

> *3 apples, cored, peeled, and sliced*
> *1 cup rolled oats*
> *1 cup whole wheat pastry flour*
> *3/4 cup apple juice*
> *3/4 cup soy milk*
> *1/4 cup maple syrup*
> *1/2 cup raisins or currants*
> *1/2 cup chopped walnuts or pistachios*
> *1/2 teaspoon cinnamon or nutmeg, or both*

Put the oats and flour in a bowl. Add the apple juice and soy milk and stir till smooth. Add the raisins, walnuts or pistachios, cinnamon, and maple syrup. Put half of this mixture in the bottom of a lightly oiled loaf pan. Add half the apples, then the other half of the mixture, followed by apples on top. Sprinkle with a little more cinnamon. Bake in a 350° oven for about 20 minutes.

Nutritional analysis per serving: 258 calories; 3.0 g fat (9.8% calories from fat); 0 mg cholesterol; 55.7 g carbohydrate; 6.0 g protein; 5 mg sodium; 44 mg calcium; 2.1mg iron; 4 mg vitamin C

LEMON TART

1 recipe rolled oat pastry
zest of 1 lemon
juice of 1 lemon (about 1/2 cup)
1/2 cup apple juice
4 tablespoons maple syrup
1 tablespoon agar flakes
1/2 cup water
2 tablespoons arrowroot
1/2 lb. silken tofu
2 tablespoons tahini (optional)
3 tablespoons maple syrup
3 tablespoons orange juice

Bake the pastry in a pie tin for about 10 minutes (see recipe for rolled oat pastry above). Meanwhile, make the filling. Remove the zest from a lemon before juicing it and grate in a processor. Put the lemon juice, the apple juice, and the 4 tablespoons of maple syrup into a small pot with the agar flakes. Bring to a slow boil, stirring until the agar dissolves. Mix the arrowroot with water until dissolved and add to the pot, stirring until the mixture thickens. Add the zest and cook for a minute more. Add the mixture to the baked crust and chill. Mix the tahini (optional), the 3 tablespoons of maple syrup, and the orange juice in a processor and add to the tart once it has set.

RASPBERRY MOUSSE

If fresh raspberries are not available, use a sugar-free raspberry spread.

1/4 cup soy milk or vanilla soy milk
1/2 cup sugar-free raspberry spread or 1 cup fresh raspberries
4 tablespoons arrowroot
3 tablespoons maple syrup
2 tablespoons agar
1 lb. silken tofu
about 1 cup more raspberries and/or blackberries and blueberries

Put the soy milk into a saucepan with the arrowroot and stir until dissolved without any heat. Add the agar and raspberry spread and bring to a simmer, stirring until they dissolve. (If using fresh raspberries, omit the spread and don't cook the raspberries.) Put all ingredients into a food processor or blender with the silken tofu, fresh raspberries (if used), and maple syrup and blend until smooth. Pour into bowls and refrigerate until set. Garnish with fresh raspberries, blackberries, or blueberries. *Serves 4 to 6*

Variation: **Strawberry Mousse**
Strawberries retain pesticides more than any other fruit or vegetable, so you want to be careful to buy organic strawberries. If they're not organic, it's best to use the spread instead. Blueberry and blackberry mousse can also be made this way.

1/2 cup soy milk or vanilla soy milk
4 tablespoons arrowroot
3 tablespoons sucanat or maple syrup
2 tablespoons agar
1 lb. silken tofu
1 cup fresh strawberries (or 1/2 cup organic sugar-free
strawberry spread and 1/2 cup strawberries)

Dissolve the arrowroot and agar in soy milk in a saucepan and bring to a simmer until thoroughly dissolved. Put into a blender or food processor with silken tofu, maple syrup, and 1/2 cup of the strawberries or 1/2 cup sugar-free strawberry spread and blend until smooth. Put into bowls and refrigerate until set. Garnish with remaining strawberries.

Serves 4 to 6

Nutritional analysis per serving for raspberry mousse: 229 calories; 4.9 g fat (18.0% calories from fat); 0 mg cholesterol; 42.0 g carbohydrate; 8.4 g protein; 22 mg sodium; 131 mg calcium; 5.6 mg iron; 15 mg vitamin C

QUICK MOUSSE

1 lb. silken tofu
4-6 tablespoons fruit spread

Silken tofu is as smooth and soft as custard, so it can be used without any extra ingredients to make a smooth, mousse-like dessert. Just add 4 tablespoons of your favorite fruit spread (or more, to your taste) to the tofu and blend in a food processor. When smoothly mixed, pour into serving bowls and chill.

Serves 4

Nutritional analysis per serving: 225 calories; 9.9g fat (37.1% calories from fat); 0 mg cholesterol; 19.9 g carbohydrate; 17.9 g protein; 16 mg sodium; 233 mg calcium; 11.9 mg iron; 0 mg vitamin C

CAROB CAKE

This dessert will make you stop yearning for rich, fatty, overly sweet cakes. You will fool people into thinking that they are having something evil, but it is all good.

> *1 cup whole wheat pastry flour*
> *1/3 cup carob powder*
> *1 tablespoon baking powder*
> *1/2 teaspoon salt*
> *1/2 cup maple syrup*
> *1/4 cup canola oil (or use 1/4 cup silken tofu to*
> * avoid the oil)*
> *1/2 cup soy milk*

> *FOR THE ICING:*
> *1/4 cup carob chips*
> *1/4 cup soy milk*

Preheat the oven to 350°. Sift the dry ingredients into a bowl and blend the maple syrup, soy milk, and oil. Add to the bowl and whisk together until smooth. Pour into a lightly oiled baking pan and bake 15 to 20 minutes. Poke with a toothpick. It's ready when it comes out dry. Let cool. Melt 1/4 cup carob chips with 1/4 cup soy milk. Stir until melted and smooth. Spread on top of the cake. You can top it with berries as well.

CAROB CAKE WITH MOUSSE TOPPING

I like the carob cake by itself, but this is heaven.

1/2 recipe carob cake
1 recipe mousse
1 pint berries

Follow the recipe for carob cake above, but cut the ingredients in half. Make one of the mousse recipes, but don't chill.

Pour the batter into a lightly oiled spring mold and bake for about five minutes. Then, carefully pour in the mousse, preventing overflow. Continue baking another 10 to 15 minutes until a tooth-pick comes out dry, then remove from the oven and let cool. When completely cool, ring the top with berries.

Nutritional analysis per serving: 2130 calories; 99.8 g fat (40.7% calories from fat); 6 mg cholesterol; 288.2 g carbohydrate; 38.2 g protein; 1322 mg sodium; 1890 mg calcium; 12.0 mg iron; 2 mg vitamin C

POACHED PEARS

There was a time when I made this dessert with a rich red wine rather than grape juice. Because alcohol evaporates in cooking, I don't think its use is terribly deleterious to your health, particularly if you don't use it daily. So if you prefer to use it, go ahead. I am providing this alternative for those who want a pure diet without a trace of harm. Some studies suggest that a glass of red wine a day is good for the heart, probably because of the flavonoids. They are also found in grape juice.

4 large, firm pears (preferably D'Anjou)
1-1/2 cups grape juice
zest of a lemon, grated
1 teaspoon cinnamon
4 tablespoons sucanat, optional

Peel the pears with a potato peeler and place in a baking dish deep enough to hold them. Pour the grape juice, lemon zest, and cinnamon over them and bake in a 350° oven until the pears are tender (about 20 minutes). The juice and the natural sweetness of the pears should be sufficient to sweeten the sauce. If you find it too bland, add a bit of sucanat to the juice.

Serves 4

Nutritional analysis per serving: 189 calories; 1.0 g fat (4.3% calories from fat); 0 mg cholesterol; 48.0 g carbohydrate; 1.4 g protein; 3 mg sodium; 42 mg calcium; 1.0 mg iron; 11 mg vitamin C

BAKED APPLES

The difference between this dish and the standard baked apple dish is that this one has no butter or any other fat. You don't need it.

4 large apples, core removed
1/2 cup apple juice
4 tablespoons maple syrup
1 tablespoon cinnamon
1 teaspoon freshly ground nutmeg
1/2 cup raisins
1/2 cup chopped walnuts

Put the apples into a non-stick baking dish just large enough to hold them. Mix the apple juice, maple syrup, cinnamon, and nutmeg and pour over apples. Sprinkle with the raisins and walnuts. Bake in a preheated 350° oven for about 20 minutes, or until soft. Put into individual bowls and serve, hot or cold.

Serves 4

Nutritional analysis per serving: 226 calories; 3.0 g fat (11.0% calories from fat); 0 mg cholesterol; 52.7 g carbohydrate; 1.9 g protein; 5 mg sodium; 64 mg calcium; 1.7 mg iron; 9 mg vitamin C

CITRUS MIXED FRUITS

1 orange
1 grapefruit
1 tart apple (Granny Smith, Macoun, Macintosh, etc.)
1 pear
1/4 cup raisins
1/4 cup apple juice
3 tablespoons maple syrup

Divide the orange and grapefruit into sections, being careful to remove the inner white of the skins, particularly on the grapefruit as it can be quite bitter. Peel, core, and slice the apples and pears. Put all of the fruit into a bowl and cover with apple juice mixed with maple syrup.

Serves 6

Nutritional analysis per serving: 154 calories; 0.5 g fat (2.7% calories from fat); 0 mg cholesterol; 39.6 g carbohydrate; 1.2 g protein; 3 mg sodium; 46 mg calcium; 0.7 mg iron; 39 mg vitamin C

MIXED BERRIES

Simple yet magnificent, particularly when the berries are in season.

1/2 pint blueberries
1/2 pint raspberries
1 pint strawberries
1/2 pint blackberries
juice of 1 lemon or lime

Mix all the berries together in a bowl and add the juice. Toss to coat. Or use whatever berries are available in the market. Rarely do they all appear at the same time.

Serves 2 to 4

Nutritional analysis per serving: 75 calories; 0.7 g fat (7.4% calories from fat); 0 mg cholesterol; 18.5 g carbohydrate; 1.2 g protein; 3 mg sodium; 30 mg calcium; 0.7 mg iron; 61 mg vitamin C

STICKY RICE WITH TROPICAL FRUITS

Mangoes and papayas are rich in beta-carotene and offset any of the negative qualities of coconut, which is higher in saturated fat than any other non-animal food. Sticky rice is glutinous and higher in starch than ordinary rice. It makes a delicious dessert.

> 1 cup sticky rice (can be found in Asian markets)
> 4 tablespoons sucanat
> 1 can unsweetened coconut milk or
>   1 cup freshly made coconut milk
> 1 mango, in small slices
> 1 banana, sliced
> 1 papaya, in small slices
> 1/2 cup grated coconut
> 1 sprig mint

Soak the rice in cold water for a few hours. Drain and put in a saucepan with the coconut milk and sucanat. It may require some extra water, about 1/2 cup. Bring to a boil and reduce heat to a slow simmer. Stir frequently until thickened. Sticky rice is usually made by steaming, so take care that it doesn't burn or stick to the pan. Add more water, if necessary. When done, put a scoop of rice into each bowl and cover with the fruits. Sprinkle with grated coconut. Place a few mint leaves on top for garnish.

> *Serves 4 to 6*

Nutritional analysis per serving: 308 calories; 11.9 g fat (33.7% calories from fat); 0 mg cholesterol; 48.9 g carbohydrate; 3.7 g protein; 26 mg sodium; 22 mg calcium; 1.4 mg iron; 30 mg vitamin C

TAPIOCA PUDDING

My mother made tapioca pudding when I was a child, but I haven't made it myself until just recently. It is a satisfying dessert option for a vegan. I've been surprised by the way it sets, requiring very little thickening in the cooking process. Most of the setting happens in refrigeration, so be careful not to let it get too thick on the stove. The pudding is versatile and can be made with many fruits, but I've found that it works best with tropical and dried fruits.

2-1/2 cups soy milk
1/2 cup tapioca pearls
3 tablespoons maple syrup
1/2 cup raisins

Bring the milk to a slow boil in a saucepan over a low heat. Add the tapioca and keep stirring. Add the maple syrup and the raisins. Stir for 5 to 10 minutes until the tapioca begins to thicken. It won't actually be thick, but will set when it is cooled. You can make tapioca without raisins. Fresh fruit such as mangoes, peaches, pineapple, and berries can be added at the last minute.

Serves 6

Nutritional analysis per serving: 138 calories; 2.0g fat (12.1% xcalories from fat); 0 mg cholesterol; 29.2 g carbohydrate; 3.2 g protein; 14 mg sodium; 23 mg calcium; 1.1 mg iron; 0 mg vitamin C

PART 111

♦ For Your Reference

MAJOR NUTRIENTS: What are they good for and where are they found?

NUTRIENT	GOOD FOR	FOUND IN
VITAMINS		
Vitamin A 5000 IU	Eyes, skin, bones, teeth, immune system, antioxidant, helps body utilize protein	alfalfa, garlic, green leafy vegetables, yellow and orange fruits and vegetables
Vitamin B1 (Thiamine)	Brain, nervous system, converts glucose to energy, helps circulation and rejuvenation of blood	green peas, rice, whole grains, corn, melon, dried beans, brown rice
Vitamin B2 (Riboflavin) 1.6 mg RDA	Red blood cell formation, antibody production, helps prevent cataracts, metabolizes carbohydrates, fats and proteins	beans, asparagus, avocados, broccoli, brussels sprouts, currants, nuts
Vitamin B3 (Niacin) 18 mg RDA	Circulation, skin, nervous system, fat and protein metabolism, lowers cholesterol, treatment of schizophrenia (may cause rash)	broccoli, carrots, corn flour, potatoes, tomatoes, whole wheat
Vitamin B5 (Pantothenic Acid) 4-7 mg RDA	Antistress vitamin, production of adrenal hormones, antibody formation	beans, fresh vegetables, whole grains
Vitamin B6 (Pyridoxine) 2 mg RDA	Absorption of fats and protein, sodium-potassium balance, red blood cell formation, RNA and DNA synthesis, boosts immune system, anticancer, anticholesterol, fights arthritis and asthma	carrots, peas, spinach, sunflower seeds, walnuts, wheat germ, avocado, bananas, beans, blackstrap molasses, brown rice and grains, cabbage, cantaloupe
Vitamin B12 3 mcg RDA	Prevents anemia, helps form cells, digestion and absorption of foods, protein synthesis, carbohydrate and fat metabolism, prevents nerve damage, helps memory	tofu, miso, tempeh, sea vegetables, spirulina

NUTRIENT	GOOD FOR	FOUND IN
Biotin 100-200 mcg RDA	Aids cell growth, carbohydrate, fat and protein metabolism, healthy hair and skin	yeast, peanut butter, whole grains, cauliflower
Choline	Nerve transmission, regulates fat metabolism in liver, hormone production	legumes, whole grain cereals
Folic acid 400 mcg RDA	Energy, red blood cell formation, DNA synthesis, protein metabolism, embryonic development	Dark leafy vegetables, broccoli, oranges, bananas, lentils, split peas, whole grains
PABA	Protects against sunburn and skin cancer	molasses, whole grains
Vitamin C 60 mg RDA	Antioxidant, cancer prevention, immune booster, collagen formation, blood clotting	green vegetables, citrus fruits, berries, melons, onions, sweet peppers, rose hips, tomatoes
Vitamin E 10 IU RDA	Protects red blood cells, neurological function, anti-oxidant, immune booster	vegetables, whole grains, nuts
Vitamin K 70-140 mcg RDA	Facilitates blood clotting	green leafy vegetables, alfalfa

MINERALS

Boron	Works with calcium to form and strengthen bones	Dried fruits; other fruits and vegetables
Calcium	Strong bones and teeth; bloodclotting; muscle, nerve and heart function	green leafy vegetables, sea vegetables, sesame seeds

NUTRIENT	GOOD FOR	FOUND IN
Chromium .05-.2 mg RDA	Insulin production and function	brewers yeast, broccoli, grape juice
Copper 2-3 mg RDA	Red blood cell formation; helps bones and nervous system, immune system	whole wheat, beans, nuts, seeds
Flouride 1.5-4 mg RDA	Bone and tooth formation	most drinking water
Iodine 150 mg RDA	Thyroid regulation	seaweed
Iron 10-18 mg RDA	Hemoglobin formation; protein metabolism	dried fruit, beans, green vegetables
Magnesium 300-400 mg RDA	Enzyme activity; bone formation; carbohydrate and mineral metabolism; regulation of mineral balance	green leafy vegetables, whole grains, apricots, bananas, tofu
Manganese 2.5-8 mg RDA	Food metabolism; nervous system, sex hormones, antioxidant, bone growth	nuts, seeds, green leafy vegetables, legumes
Phosphorous 800-1200 mg RDA	bones and teeth; cell growth; converts food to energy; forms genetic material, cell membranes, enzymes	most foods, esp. bran, corn, garlic, legumes, whole grains, pumpkin seeds
Potassium 800-1200 mg RDA	Nervous system; heart regulation; muscle contraction; blood pressure regulation	most fruits, vegetables and whole grains, esp. apricots, avocados, bananas, garlic, potatoes
Selenium .08-2 mg RDA	Antioxidant, free radical scavenger; pancreatic function	whole grains, garlic, onion, broccoli, Brazil nuts

NUTRIENT	GOOD FOR	FOUND IN
Sodium 1100-3300 mg RDA	Fluid balance; stomach, nerve and muscle function	virtually all foods
Zinc 18 mg RDA	Cell division, growth, repair; prostate function; maintains taste, smell; protein synthesis	legumes, whole grains, lima beans, mushrooms, pumpkin seeds, soybeans

PHYTOCHEMICALS

NUTRIENT	GOOD FOR	FOUND IN
Capsaicin	Anti-inflammatory and pain relieving; lowers cholesterol	chili peppers
Carotenoids (Vitamin A precursors)	Antioxidants; cell differentiation agents; anticarcinogenic	parsley, carrots, winter squash, sweet potatoes, yams, cantaloupe, apricots, spinach, kale, turnip greens, citrus fruits
• Alpha-Carotene	Fights lung cancer, improves immune system	carrots, pumpkin
• Beta-Carotene	Antioxidant; fights cancer, stroke; improves immune system; lowers cholesterol; helps prevent cardiovascular disease	dried apricots and peaches, carrots, dill, pumpkin, fennel, parsley, red pepper, spinach, sweet potato, Swiss chard, watermelon, red and yellow fruits and vegetables, green leafy vegetables
• Lycopene	Antioxidant, fights prostate and digestive tract cancers (stomach, rectal, colon) and cervical cancer	tomatoes, especially cooked (with some oil), pink grapefruit, watermelon, scallion,
Catechins	Antioxidants; fight gastrointestinal cancers; antiviral	green tea, berries
Coumarins	Blood thinners-fight heart disease and strokes; anticarcinogenic	parsley, licorice, cereal grains, citrus fruits, other fruits and vegetables

NUTRIENT	GOOD FOR	FOUND IN
Ellagic Acid	Anticarcinogenic	cherries, grapes, strawberries
Flavonoids	Block receptors for carcinogenic hormones; prevent heart disease; antioxidants	parsley, carrots, citrus, broccoli, cabbage, squash, yams, red grapes, tomatoes, berries, pepper
• Genistein	Blocks blood vessels that feed tumors	soy products, some cabbages
• Isoflavones	Block estrogen receptors, fighting breast cancer	legumes- kidney beans, peas, lentils; peanuts
Indoles	Stimulate protective enzymes; help prevent breast and other cancers	cabbage, brussels sprouts, kale
Lignans	Antioxidants; fight breast cancer	flax seed
Phenols	antioxidants, protect DNA, affect enzyme activity	parsley, carrots, broccoli, cabbage, tomatoes, eggplant, peppers, whole grains, citrus, berries
Protease inhibitors	AIDS fighters, block excessive proteins, anticarcinogenic	soybeans, kidney beans, chickpeas, tofu, whole grains, esp. flax and oats
Sulphur Compounds	Anticarcinogenic, antibacterial, antifungal	onions, garlic, scallions, leeks, radishes, mustard
• Allylic sulfides	Anticarcinogenic, antioxidant, lower cholesterol, help immune system	garlic and onions
• Isothiocyanates	Stimulate protective enzymes	mustard, horseradish, radishes
• Sulforaphane	Enhance enzymes that block carcinogens	broccoli, brussels sprouts, kale, scallions, cauliflower

NUTRIENT	GOOD FOR	FOUND IN
Terpinoids	Help lungs; stimulate anticarcinogenic enzymes	citrus fruits, parsnip
• Limonoids	Stimulate protective enzymes	citrus fruits and rinds
• Monoterpines	Antioxidants; inhibit cholesterol; aid protective enzymes	parsley, carrots, cabbage, broccoli, cucumbers, squash, yams, tomatoes, eggplant, peppers, citrus, mint, basil

Favored Foods: Nutritional Values Per 100 Gram Serving

VEGETABLES	Calories	IU Vit A	mg Vit B1	mg Vit B2	mg Vit B3	mg Vit B5	mg Vit B6	mcg biotin	mcg folic acid	mg Vit C	IU Vit E
adzuki beans (1 cup=197 g)	326	16	.5	.1	2.5	na	.33	na	587	0	na
artichoke	18	60	.025	.016	.2	.118	.038	na	12	3.1	.006
asparagus	15	655	.115	.13	1	.309	.056	.5	57	19	1.5
beets	30	16	.022	.036	.12	.107	na	na	71.2	5.24	.026
black beans (1 cup=194 g)	339	30	.56	.2	2.2	na	.27	na	419.4	0	na
blackeye peas (1 cup=167 g)	318	47	.8	.22	.05	.9	.34	na	598	1	na
bok choy	13	3003	.04	.07	.5	na	.16	na	54.6	.08	45
broccoli	19.6	2235	.07	.13	.5	.6	.18	na	65.1	88	28
brussels sprouts	45	930	.14	.24	1.56	1	.4	na	73	175	65
burdock	75	.3	.05	.02	.2	na	.17	na	16.1	na	na
cabbage, green	25	247	.05	.5	.4	.2	.145	na	32	48	.29
cabbage, red	28	41	.78	.057	.4	.35	.204	na	37.4	67	.22
carrot	34	27848	.04	.039	.48	.19	.11	2.7	22.9	5.99	.35
cauliflower	23	16	.076	.058	.632	.14	.23	1.5	6.6	71	.15
celery	15	134	.031	.031	.31	.19	.031	.1	10.1	7.1	.54
chard	23	3290	.038	.088	.38	.17	.08	na	7.5	.12	29.9
chickpeas (1 cup=200 g)	360	50	.31	.15	2	na	.51	na	525.5	.19	6
collards	40	3326	.028	.639	.37	.64	.67	na	11.5	16.64	.368
corn	53	280	.135	.058	1.68	.759	.054	1.26	45.4	6.87	na
cucumber	14	46	.032	.02	.321	.26	.054	1	14.4	4.8	8.4
eggplant	25	70.8	.09	.019	.6	.08	.095	na	17.56	.17	na
endive	15	2052	.08	.076	.4	.9	.2	na	142	6.4	na
garlic (1 clove= avg. 3 g)	136	0	.31	0	.6	na	.94	na	2.5	3.3	na
ginger	50	10	.2	.04	.7	na	na	na	na	4	na
green beans	30	662	.83	.11	.75	.98	.78	na	36	16	.09
Jerusalem artichoke	66	19.8	.2	.06	1.28	na	.05	na	8.7	3.96	na
kale	40	8885	.11	.13	.99	.09	.29	.75	29.2	120	11.9
kidney beans (1 cup= 184 g.)	117	5.4	.1	.05	.7	na	.37	na	372.1	.03	3
leeks	52	96	.059	.02	.4	.097	.17	1.13	64.4	12	.8
lentils, cooked	106	20	.07	.06	.6	na	.17	na	170.7	1	na

VEGETABLES	calcium mg	iron mg	magns mg	mangns mg	phos mg	potas mg	sodium mg	zinc mg	fat g	fiber g	carbo g	protein g
adzuki beans	7.5	4.8	na	na	350	1,500	20	4.8	1.6	4.3	58.4	21.5
artichoke	20	.41	10.8	.4	90	120	12	.128	.06	1.3	3.96	1.1
asparagus	15	1.5	7.25	.286	na	155	4	.438	.15	1.08	2.6	1.6
beets	18.2	.72	16.8	.4	na	284	72	.36	.11	2.67	6.42	1.33
black beans (dry)	135	7.9	na	na	420	1,038	25	3.4	1.5	14.4	22.3	22.3
blackeye peas	104	7.8	110	na	300	1051	15	3.2	1.2	10	56.7	22.2
bok choy	104.8	.8	18.59	na	37.2	251	64.35	.2	.2	.6	2.2	1.5
broccoli	76	.79	15	.25	na	187	15.5	.23	.28	5.4	2.7	2.76
brussels sprouts	930	1.95	38.2	na	na	484	19.5	.76	.78	5.85	8.2	7
burdock	47	.8	na	na	71	218	45	.2	.1	2.3	4.2	4.1
cabbage, green	62	.8	10.4	na	na	234	16	.49	.3	2	4.75	2
cabbage, red	47.3	.61	17.8	na	na	223	28	.39	.3	2	4.75	2
carrot	27	.37	13.3	.149	43	231	34	.32	.13	3.6	5.82	.667
cauliflower	.51	.58	14	.2	46	356	14	.18	.18	.82	4.9	1.98
celery	38.7	.51	12.3	.144	30	299	103	.18	.13	.68	3.8	.66
chard	49.9	1.77	38.7	1.25	44.3	376	210	.3	.08	.77	3.7	1.77
chickpeas (dry)	150	6.9	na	na	331	340	26	2.7	5.7	1.5	21.4	7.8
collards	117	.62	16.1	.24	8.59	73	27.9	.96	.4	.537	3.76	1.56
corn	2.59	.52	37.6	.16	89.5	270	14.9	.45	1.7	.65	10	3.22
cucumber	14	.28	12	.064	18	156	2	.24	.14	.62	3	.56
eggplant	36.6	.84	15	.122	31.7	220	.05	.1	.09	1	6.1	1.09
endive	52	.84	16	.42	22	316	24	.8	.12	.52	3.36	1.24
garlic	34	1.3	33.3	na	200	532	33	1.26	.66	16.7	30	6.6
ginger	23	2.1	na	na	36	264	6	.2	1	1.1	9.5	1.4
green beans	37	1.02	24.3	.21	37.8	207	5.4	.234	.01	1.08	7.1	1.8
Jerusalem artichoke	13.9	3.4	17.2	.06	na	77.3	3	.1	.01	.79	17.2	2
kale	134	1.7	34.3	.773	56.6	445	43	.43	.7	1.49	9.98	3.29
kidney beans	37.8	2.4	na	na	140	340	23	2.6	.5	1.5	21	7.8
leeks	25	.9	15	.006	125	75	8	.1	.1	.7	5.1	.6
lentils (cooked)	25	2.1	na	na	119	249	30	1	t	1.2	19.3	7.8

VEGETABLES	Calories	IU Vit A	mg Vit B1	mg Vit B2	mg Vit B3	mg Vit B5	mg Vit B6	mcg biotin	mcg folic acid	mg Vit C	IU Vit E
lentils, dry (1 cup=192 g)	319	37	.45	.23	2.5	na	.51	na	408.6	6	na
lettuce	6	2606	.1	.1	.42	.5	.03	na	30.1	136	24
lima beans (1 cup=178 g.)	138	30	.13	.05	.68	na	.18	na	.04	1	na
mung beans	35	19	.13	.13	.76	na	na	na	na	.008	19
mushrooms	27	0	.102	.43	4.12	2.2	.13	na	21.2	3.43	.83
okra	38	660	.2	.06	1	.246	.2	na	88	21	na
onions	34	0	.06	.01	.1	.125	.156	.937	19.87	8.37	.25
parsley	44	8466	.116	.265	1.16	.298	11.2	.398	.116	171	na
parsnips	64	32.2	.07	.08	.129	.58	.09	.096	.058	10.3	na
peas	71	538	.28	.11	2.3	.34	.35	na	20	38	na
peppers, hot	40	705	.09	.09	.948	.061	.279	na	23.27	242	na
peppers, sweet	30	530	.086	.05	.54	16.6	1.64	na	.036	128	na
potato	61	t	.099	.039	1.5	.376	.18	na	9.1	12.6	19.8
pumpkin	26	1087	.031	.07	.11	.41	.57	na	.019	4.7	na
radish	15	6.6	.004	.044	.29	.08	.07	na	26.8	22.6	na
rutabaga	46	575	.071	.071	1.06	.156	.1	na	.026	42.6	na
scallions	26	5000	.07	.14	.2	.144	.05	na	58	13.8	45
SEA VEGETABLES											
agar	25	0	0	0	0	0	.03	na	80.1	0	na
arame	311	50	na	na	na	na	na	na	na	na	na
hijiki	242	150	.01	.2	3	0	0	0	na	0	0
kombu	43	430	.88	.32	1.8	na	na	na	na	10	na
nori (1 sheet 2.8 g)	360	11,000	.25	1.24	10	na	0	na	0	6344	na
wakame	45	140	.11	.14	1	na	0	na	184.6	15	na
soybeans	130	27	.21	.1	.6	na	.36	na	354.1	6	na
spinach	10	8082	.108	.198	.54	.27	.25	6.3	.19	50.54	2.25
squash, winter	30	4133	.048	.129	.62	.268	.086	na	14.5	12.9	na
sweet potato	92	20,083	.066	.147	.674	.59	.257	na	13.8	23.1	na
tomato	22	1129	.059	.05	.597	.246	.047	1.62	9.3	17.5	.44

VEGETABLES	calcium mg	iron mg	magns mg	mangns mg	phos mg	potas mg	sodium mg	zinc mg	fat g	fiber g	carbo g	protein g
lentils, dry	48	8.5	na	na	na	854	9	3.4	.9	28.8	53.9	26.5
lettuce	35.8	1.1	7.16	na	46	290	7.2	.2	.72	2.31	1.6	6
lima beans	29	3.1	na	na	154	612	2.7	.89	.6	1.6	25.6	8.2
mung beans	19	1.3	na	na	64	223	5	.86	.2	.67	6.6	3.8
mushrooms	5.72	1.23	11.4	na	103	372	2.86	.49	.43	2.23	2.08	27
okra	82	.8	56	.99	64	302	8	.6	1	.94	7.6	2
onions	25	.36	10	.25	28.7	156	2.5	.2	.26	.44	7.3	1.17
parsley	203	6.14	40.6	.934	63	727	44.8	.73	.26	1.49	8.46	3.62
parsnips	45	.58	25.8	.48	62	379	7.74	.51	.34	1.93	14.8	64
peas	11	1.8	na	na	99	136	1.3	.75	.4	.4	12.1	5.4
peppers, hot	17.3	1.19	25.27	.236	45.2	339	6.65	.305	.19	1.79	9.3	2
peppers, sweet	6	1.2	14	.14	22	196	4	.18	.46	1.2	5.3	.86
potato	7.26	.059	33.6	.26	52.6	403	3.3	.38	.13	.435	17	2.1
pumpkin	30.3	.574	9	na	30.3	231	1.23	.2	.07	.82	4.9	.76
radish	19.8	.286	8.8	.07	17.6	229	24.2	.28	.52	.52	3.52	.59
rutabaga	65.3	.426	14.2	.04	39	238	49.7	.34	.2	1	11	1.06
scallions	60	1.88	20	na	32	256	4	.44	.14	.84	5.5	1.7

SEA VEGETABLES

	calcium mg	iron mg	magns mg	mangns mg	phos mg	potas mg	sodium mg	zinc mg	fat g	fiber g	carbo g	protein g
agar	400	5	na	na	8	213	8	.5	.1	0	.75	2.3
arame	1,170	12	na	na	150	na	na	na	60	na	na	na
hijiki	1,400	29	na	na	59	14,800	0	0	0	13	42.3	5.6
kombu	800	10	na	na	150	5,800	2500	na	1.1	3	52	7.3
nori	260	12	na	na	510	3,800	600	0	.7	4.7	44	35.6
wakame	1,300	13	na	na	260	2,700	2,500	.4	.6	3.6	51.4	12.7
soybeans	72.8	2.7	na	na	179	540	2.2	4.6	5.7	1.7	10.7	11
spinach	91.8	3.06	79.2	na	50.4	466	70	.9	.36	.54	4.32	3.29
squash, winter	27.4	.768	6.72	.35	47	454	.48	.16	.19	1.2	15.2	1.8
sweet potato	22.3	.585	10.7	.142	28.4	204	13	.27	.29	.77	24.6	1.54
tomato	6.44	.477	11.3	.648	23.4	205	.8	.105	.21	.46	4.2	.89

VEGETABLES	Calories	IU Vit A	mg Vit B1	mg Vit B2	mg Vit B3	mg Vit B5	mg Vit B6	mcg biotin	mcg folic acid	mg Vit C	IU Vit E
turnip	25	t	.038	.069	.61	.2	.09	.4	.02	36.2	.02
water chestnut	61	0	.16	.2	.8	na	.24	na	11.7	4	na
white beans	115	0	.6	.27	.28	na	.6	na	739.6	0	na
zucchini	16	408	.053	.092	1	.36	.143	na	.03	22.3	na

GRAINS

	Calories	IU Vit A	mg Vit B1	mg Vit B2	mg Vit B3	mg Vit B5	mg Vit B6	mcg biotin	mcg folic acid	mg Vit C	IU Vit E
arrowroot	337	0	0	0	0	na	.01	na	6	0	na
barley (1 cup=184 g)	349	0	.17	.05	3.1	na	.3	na	20	0	na
buckwheat (1 cup=120 g)	333	0	.6	.15	29	1.5	.2	na	28.3	0	33
bulgur (1 cup= 140 g)	358	0	.278	.139	4.5	.65	.22	na	4.46	0	na
cornmeal (1 cup= 138 g)	355	481	.283	.076	1.87	.55	.246	na	16	0	na
gluten	379	0	na	na	na	na	na	na	na	na	na
millet (1 cup cooked= 138 g)	326	0	.73	.38	2.3	na	.578	na	50	0	1.9
oats (1 cup= 150 g)	313	0	.3	.10	1.5	na	.11	na	52.9	0	1
rice, brown (1 cup=190g)	360	0	.34	.04	4.7	na	.5	na	18.9	0	na
rye flour (1 cup= 102 g)	330	na	.43	.22	1.6	na	.25	na	17.9	0	na
soy flour (1 cup= 85 g)	273	71	.544	.198	1.35	1.09	.43	44	280	0	na
w w flour (1 cup= 120 g)	334	0	.547	.116	4.31	1.09	.34	4.98	54	0	2.59
wild rice (1 cup= 160 g)	352	0	.45	.63	6.2	1.01	.37	na	89.7	0	na

FRUITS & NUTS

	Calories	IU Vit A	mg Vit B1	mg Vit B2	mg Vit B3	mg Vit B5	mg Vit B6	mcg biotin	mcg folic acid	mg Vit C	IU Vit E
almonds (1 cup= 142 g)	600	0	.238	.12	.23	1.6	.099	na	.122	t	14.9
apple	152	142	.43	.035	.199	.16	.13	na	7.48	4.9	1.47
apricot	47.8	2760	.29	.039	.630	.25	.5	na	8.8	10.1	.9
avocado	120	347	.06	.069	1.09	.55	.05	na	35	4.5	.75
banana	56	49	.027	.06	.33	.027	.156	na	12.7	5.45	.21
blackberries (1 cup= 144 g)	55	320	.05	.78	.77	.46	.113	na	66	40.8	1.16
blueberries (1 cup= 145 g)	57	100	.05	.05	.36	.093	.036	na	6.4	13	na
Brazil nuts (1 cup= 140 g)	650	t	.95	.12	1.56	.229	.169	na	.004	9.94	6.46
cantaloupe	20	1807	.02	.012	.064	.32	.05	1.2	8.2	5.5	.056
cashews (1 cup= 130 g)	562	100	.43	.25	1.8	1.3	.004	na	.63	0	na

VEGETABLES	calcium mg	iron mg	magns mg	mangns mg	phos mg	potas mg	sodium mg	zinc mg	fat g	fiber g	carbo g	protein g
turnip	39.3	.539	19.2	.04	30	268	.1	.2	.1	.88	6.6	1
water chestnut	4	.8	9.6	na	64	500	20	.4	.4	.8	19.2	1.6
white beans	200	10.5	na	na	570	1590	27	3.9	2.3	7	82	40
zucchini	27.7	.385	16.1	na	29	202	.77	.25	.21	.57	4.23	1.07

GRAINS

	calcium mg	iron mg	magns mg	mangns mg	phos mg	potas mg	sodium mg	zinc mg	fat g	fiber g	carbo g	protein g
arrowroot	337	.3	na	na	na	10	2	.1	.1	3.2	83.2	.3
barley	16	2	35.7	na	189	160	3	2.6	1.4	.4	79	8.2
buckwheat	33	5	na	2.09	347	656	1	2.3	2.4	9.9	72.5	11.7
bulgur	28	3.64	na	333	226	387	16	1.8	1.5	1.74	75	11.2
cornmeal	17	1.78	106	na	224	249	.85	1.78	3.4	1	75	9
gluten	40	na	na	na	139	60	2.13	na	1.9	.42	47	41
millet	20	6.8	162	na	311	430	6	2.5	2.9	3.2	73	9.9
oats	55	4.6	na	na	320	0	10	14	5.4	10.6	66	13
rice, brown	32	1.6	88	216	220	216	9	1.8	1.8	.9	77.4	7.5
rye flour	38	3.7	115	na	376	467	1	1.9	1.7	2	73.4	12.2
soy flour	129	.54	160	na	362	1,076	.9	na	13	1.5	19.7	23.6
whole wheat flour	40.7	3.32	113	6.4	370	369	3.32	2.4	2	2.32	72	13.3
wild rice	17.4	3.87	90.7	na	341	222	6.9	5.6	.69	.875	76	14.2

FRUITS & NUTS

	calcium mg	iron mg	magns mg	mangns mg	phos mg	potas mg	sodium mg	zinc mg	fat g	fiber g	carbo g	protein g
almonds	234	4.3	271	1.8	504	773	4	5.1	54	2.6	19.5	18.6
apple	19.2	.48	11.5	na	na	305	1.9	.09	.94	8.2	40.3	.92
apricot	14.6	.54	7.5	na	na	308	.8	.24	.38	2	11.2	1.39
avocado	6.1	.56	22.2	na	na	339	6	.24	8.7	1.7	4	1.15
banana	5.09	.187	17.2	na	na	239	.53	.1	.29	2.04	14.2	.63
blackberries	31.9	.576	20	1.28	20.7	195	0	.27	.39	4.07	12.6	.72
blueberries	6.2	.165	4.83	.28	10.35	89	6.2	.11	.38	1.3	14.2	.67
Brazil nuts	184	3.4	249	2.02	689	711	.71	5.04	66	2.98	10.9	14.2
cantaloupe	5.88	.05	5.88	.026	9.45	173	4.8	.086	.03	.2	4.63	.49
cashews	38	3.8	267	na	373	464	15	4.35	46	1.4	29.3	17.2

FRUITS & NUTS	Calories	IU Vit A	mg Vit B1	mg Vit B2	mg Vit B3	mg Vit B5	mg Vit B6	mcg biotin	mcg folic acid	mg Vit C	IU Vit E
cherries (1 cup= 155 g)	47	214	.05	.06	.4	.127	.035	.35	4.2	7.38	na
chestnuts (1 cup= 145 g)	194	0	.22	.22	.6	.47	.33	na	43.3	6	.5
coconut	345	0	.05	.025	.5	.2	.044	na	.038	2.5	1
cranberries (1 cup= 110 g)	44	46	.3	.2	.210	.1	.068	na	1.8	13.4	na
dates	273	50.4	.09	.1	2.18	.776	.19	na	12.48	0	na
figs	79	140	.058	.049	.39	.29	.11	na	5.6	2	na
filberts (1 cup= 144 g)	634	107	.46	.05	.9	.96	.5	na	.07	0	na
grapefruit	19	61.8	.018	.124	.05	.14	.02	na	5.03	1.71	.108
grapes	43	73	.09	.056	.3	.023	.11	na	7	10.8	na
lemon	20	20	.019	.018	.62	.75	.052	na	9	41	na
mango	44	2660	.04	.018	.5	.113	.1	1.98	15	37	.09
nectarine	59	660	.015	.037	.57	na	.022	na	3.2	33.6	na
orange	35	148	.06	.028	.2	.18	.043	.99	21.8	38.3	.236
peach	33	404	.013	.03	.748	.128	.014	1.38	2.6	4.95	na
peanuts (1 cup= 146 g)	564	t	1.14	.13	17.2	2.08	.495	na	.07	0	na
pear	55	18	.018	.036	.09	.06	.016	.11	6.65	3.63	na
pecans (1 cup= 108 g)	687	130	.86	.13	.9	1.6	.169	na	.024	1.85	52
pineapple	52	22.57	.092	.036	.42	.16	.087	na	10.8	15.4	na
pine nuts (1 tbs= 10 g)	642	35.7	1.3	.25	4.7	na	.09	na	41.6	t	na
pistachios (1 cup= 128 g)	587	229	.7	.174	1.4	na	.12	na	.06	3	na
pumpkin seeds (1 cup= 64 g)	553	71	.24	.314	2.4	na	.24	na	.102	0	na
raisins (1 cup= 145 g)	289	0	.113	.183	1.12	.179	.184	.427	3.1	18.78	na
raspberries (1 cup= 123 g)	50	130	.029	.089	.89	.238	.056	1.85	23.6	24.9	na
sesame seeds (1 cup= 144 g)	553	30	.98	.24	5.4	.686	.083	na	90.6	0	na
strawberries	37	27.5	.02	.065	.22	.339	.059	1.07	17.68	56.6	na
sunflower seeds (1 cup= 144 g)	560	50	1.96	.23	5.4	1.74	1.25	na	115.9	0	na
tangerine	34	665	.075	.015	.115	.14	.048	na	14.7	22.36	na
walnuts (1 cup= 125 g)	651	30	.33	.13	.9	.9	.73	.37	.06	2	1.5
watermelon	26	381	.08	.02	.2	.21	.144	3.44	2.12	9.6	na

FRUITS & NUTS	calcium mg	iron mg	magns mg	mangns mg	phos mg	potas mg	sodium mg	zinc mg	fat g	fiber g	carbo g	protein g
cherries	14.5	.38	11	na	19.3	224	.69	.006	.96	.4	16.6	1.2
chestnuts	27	1.7	53.6	na	88	454	6	.4	1.5	1.1	42.1	2.9
coconut	12.5	1.7	46.3	na	95	256	22.5	1.1	35	3.37	9.37	3.8
cranberries	7.35	.2	5.2	.15	8.3	70.3	1.05	.16	.2	1.16	13	.38
dates	32.4	1.15	34.8	.3	39.6	649	2.4	.29	.44	2.19	73.2	1.95
figs	33.8	.35	16.9	.126	13.9	228	1.54	.138	.29	1.18	18.8	.74
filberts	20.9	3.4	233	4.8	337	454	2	2.6	62	3	16.7	12.6
grapefruit	5.81	.04	4.15	.15	8.3	69.3	0	.037	.05	.09	4.02	.31
grapes	10.6	.25	6.25	na	13.1	185	1.87	.056	.57	2	17.75	.66
lemon	18	.4	2	na	na	85	2	.07	.18	1.2	5.6	.7
mango	9.24	.18	9.24	.04	7.26	106	7.59	.135	.18	.57	11.55	.339
nectarine	36.3	1.71	16.5	na	35	171	9.24	.1	.4	.376	10.6	.84
orange	28.6	.07	7.15	.018	9.9	130	0	.066	.08	.31	8.47	.67
peach	4.35	.086	5.2	.036	4.56	149	0	.104	.07	.486	8.38	.53
peanuts	69	2.1	175	na	401	674	5	2	48	2.4	18.6	26
pear	10.5	2.02	32	.314	9.9	144	.55	.11	.36	1.27	13.8	.36
pecans	73	2.4	131	1.42	289	603	.43	5.8	7.1	2.3	14.6	9.2
pineapple	7.09	.367	13.5	1.64	7.09	113	.645	.077	.43	.54	12.4	.387
pine nuts	10.7	5.36	na	na	610	606	3.57	4.31	51	1.1	20.7	13.2
pistachios	131	7.3	158	na	500	987	5.46	1.3	54	2	8.7	13.3
ppumpkin seeds	51	11.2	524	na	1,144	868	17	9.7	47	1.9	15	29
raisins	16.5	.427	13.4	.75	9.15	114	0	.35	.41	.677	7.87	2.54
raspberries	21.9	.567	17.8	1	12.2	151	0	.46	.55	2.98	11.5	.89
sesame seeds	1,160	10.5	180	na	616	725	17	7.3	47	1.9	15	29
strawberries	14.1	.038	10.7	.29	18.8	166	1.34	.127	.37	.53	6.96	.61
sunflower seeds	120	7.1	49.5	33.3	837	920	30	6.34	47	3.8	19.9	24
tangerine	10.3	.07	.86	.29	6.88	113	.8	.2	.14	.24	8.08	.43
walnuts	99	3.1	131	1.8	380	450	2	2.26	64	2.1	15.8	14.8
watermelon	8.1	.175	10.6	.023	8.75	116	1.87	.068	.42	.3	7.18	.62

MEAT & FISH

A selection of dairy, meat, and fish is given as a contrast to the above. Meats vary according to the cut, so I have given an average.

	Calories	Vit A	Vit B1	Vit B2	Vit B3	Vit B5	Vit B6	Vit B12	Biotin	Folicin	Vit C	Vit E	Chol.
beef	259	48.4	.11	.19	3.05	.3	.376	2.76	na	6.6	0	na	69.4
lamb	238	0	.12	.19	3.96	.44	.231	1.8	na	3.96	0	.79	59.4
pork	260	.06	.72	.195	4.5	.66	.398	.62	na	7.26	.7	na	73
veal (cutlet)	150	0	.116	.21	5.32	.71	.268	1.25	4.99	5.06	0	na	56
chicken	186	99	.058	.086	8.8	.62	.48	.335	na	3.44	2.9	na	17
duck	403	169	.2	.21	.39	.95	.19	.25	na	13	2.8	na	48
bass	96	94	.105	.035	2.2	.54	.11	3.8	na	14.2	2	na	79.6
bluefish	123	395	.051	.072	5.24	.748	.356	5.36	na	1.9	0	na	58.5
sole, flounder	91	32.7	.08	.07	2.8	.24	.2	1.5	na	0	1.5	na	48
salmon	142	39.8	.22	37.4	7.8	1.6	.813	3.16	1.98	3.8	9.6	na	55
whole milk	61.5	126	.038	.16	.084	.304	.042	.357	2.05	4.92	.939	.12	13.5
2 eggs	158	520	.088	.30	.062	1.74	.12	1.55	2.2	64	na	1.14	548
butter (1 T)	101	433	0	.004	.006	0	0	0	0	.375	0	223	31
butter (100 g)	717	3071	0	.028	.043	0	0	0	0	na	0	1.6	220

MEAT & FISH

The amount of copper in animal products is more significant than in vegetables, and thus is included in this chart.

	calcium	copper	iron	magn	mang	phos	potass	sodium	zinc	fat	protein
beef	7.48	.08	2.24	19.6	.008	176	293	51.8	3.41	20	18.2
lamb	7.7	.05	1.03	13.2	na	121	220	48.4	1.1	19.8	13.8
pork	5.5	.07	1.03	.12	na	19	308	48	1.9	21	13.8
veal (cutlet)	9.02	.25	2.39	16	na	161	255	55.6	2	9.02	15.9
chicken	11	.059	.96	20.6	.005	.62	204	65	.93	11	20
duck	10.5	.236	2.4	14.7	na	139	210	63.6	1.36	40	11.5
bass	76	.03	.83	na	.015	204	271	69	.39	2.32	17.7
bluefish	7.02	.058	.54	32.8	.022	226	370	60	.807	4.2	20
sole, flounder	17.5	.032	.49	31.6	.016	182	359	80.7	.45	1.17	18.7
salmon	11.7	.21	.79	30.6	.01	199	488	43.3	.5	6.3	19.7
whole milk	119	.02	.042	13.5	.002	93.4	152	49.2	.38	3.34	3.29
2 eggs	56	.2	2.08	12	.058	180	130	138	1.44	11.2	12
butter (1 T)	3.37	.004	.022	.25	.006	3.25	3.62	117	.007	11.5	.12
butter (100 g)	26.8	.028	.156	1.77	.043	23	25.7	831	.049	81.6	.85

OILS (1 tbs=13.5 g)	Vit E	calcium	copper	iron	phos	zinc	saturated fat	unsat fat	calories
canola–1 tbs	na	0	na	na	0	na	1	14	120
100 g	na	na	na	0	na	na	7.35	103	885
corn–1 tbs	11.3	0	na	0	na	.025	1.7	11.3	120
100g	83	na	na	na	na	1.3	12.5	83	885
olive–1 tbs	1.7	.02	.01	.05	.16	.01	1.8	11	119
100 g	12.5	.147	.074	.368	1.18	.074	13.6	81	875
peanut–1 tbs	3.4	.01	.001	0	na	0	2.35	10.5	119
100 g	25	.074	.007	na	na	na	17.3	77.2	875
safflower–1 tbs	5.2	0	na	0	na	.18	1.2	11.7	120
100 g	38.2	na	na	na	na	1.33	8.82	86	885
sesame–1 tbs	4	0	.056	0	na	.18	1.9	11	120
100 g	29.4	na	.41	na	na	1.33	14	81	885
soy–1 tbs	12.7	.01	na	.03	.01	na	2	11	120
100 g	93.3	.074	na	.022	na	.074	14.7	81	885
sunflower–1 tbs	34.6	0	na	0	na	.52	1.4	11.7	120
100 g	254	na	na	na	na	3.82	10.29	86	885

BIBLIOGRAPHY

Appleton, Nancy. *Secrets of Natural Healing with Food*. Rudra Press, 1995.

Balch, James F. and Phyllis A. *Prescription for Nutritional Healing*. Avery Publishing Group, 1990.

Barnard, Neal. *Food for Life*. Crown Publishers, 1993.

Bhumichitr, Vatcharin. *Thai Vegetarian Cooking*. Asia Books, 1991.

Bryant, Barry. *Cancer and Consciousness*. Sigo Press, 1990.

Chopra, Deepak. *Quantum Healing*. Bantam New Age, 1989.

Devi, Yamuna. *The Best of Lord Krishna's Cuisine*. Bala Books, 1991.

Dunne, Lavon. *Nutrition Almanac*. McGraw Hill Publishing Co., 1990.

Jacobson, Michael, Lefferts, Lisa and Garland, Anne Witte. *Safe Food: Eating Wisely in a Risky World*. Living Planet Press, 1991.

Kradjian, Robert. *Save Yourself from Breast Cancer*. Berkeley Books, 1994.

Kushi, Aveline, with Esko, Wendy. *The Macrobiotic Cancer Prevention Cookbook*. Avery Publishing Group, 1988.

Mindell, Earl. *Earl Mindell's Food as Medicine*. Fireside Books, 1994.

Mitchell, Keith. *Practically Macrobiotic*. Healing Arts Press, 1988.

New York Times. Many articles about recent research in food and nutrition were sources of information about this book.

Null, Gary. *Vegetarian Cooking for Good Health*. Collier Books, 1991.

Pickarski, Ron. *Friendly Foods*. 10 Speed Press, 1991.

Robertson, Laurel; Flinders, Carol; and Ruppenthal, Brian. *Laurel's Kitchen*. 10 Speed Press, 1986.

Sahni, Julie. *Classic Indian Vegetarian and Grain Cooking*. William Morrow, 1985.

Simone, Charles B. *Cancer and Nutritition*. Avery Publishing Group, 1992.

Turner, Lisa. *Meals that Heal*. Healing Arts Press, 1996.

Wagner, Lindsay and Spade, Ariane. *High Road to Health*. Fireside Books, 1990.

Weil, Andrew. *Spontaneous Healing*. Alfred Knopf, 1995.

INDEX